IMAGES
of America

DOUGLASVILLE

IMAGES
of America

DOUGLASVILLE

Lisa Cooper

ARCADIA
PUBLISHING

Published by Arcadia Publishing
Charleston, South Carolina

Library of Congress Control Number: 2013955789

For all general information, please contact Arcadia Publishing:
Telephone 843-853-2070
Fax 843-853-0044
E-mail sales@arcadiapublishing.com
For customer service and orders:
Toll-Free 1-888-313-2665

Visit us on the Internet at www.arcadiapublishing.com

To the citizens of the city of Douglasville—past, present, and future

CONTENTS

Acknowledgments   6

Introduction   7

1.   From Skint Chestnut to Douglasville   9

2.   Courthouse, Railroad, and Cotton Mill   13

3.   City Government and Law Enforcement   35

4.   Hospitals, Churches, and Schools   43

5.   Downtown Business District   65

6.   People, Homes, and Events   97

Bibliography   126

Index   127

ACKNOWLEDGMENTS

While I have been writing seriously since 2006, Douglas County history has consumed most of my time since 2010. A good friend of mine named Richard Segal suggested I answer a call for writers at *Douglasville Patch*. I'm forever grateful to the *Patch's* former editor, John Barker, for taking a chance on me. Another journalist I'm forever grateful to is Mitch Sneed, editor at the *Douglas County Sentinel*. My weekly column began appearing in the paper in March 2013, opening me up to a much wider audience, which in turn broadened my ability to find out more of the Douglas County story.

A huge thank you goes out to Mayor Harvey Persons, who granted me full access to the city's photograph collection. Stephanie Aylworth and her staff have my undying thanks for their assistance. Wes Tallon also opened the county's photographs to me as well.

Many thanks go to the folks willing to share their stories, memories, impressions, and opinions with me regarding Douglasville history, including my many friends on the "Every Now and Then" page on Facebook. My friend Bob Smith has been invaluable to me for support and direction on various aspects of history, including time lines and how things fit together. Judge Robert James is another who has taken his valuable time to share stories, documents, and photographs from his collection. Brian Stout, a volunteer at the Douglas County Museum of History and Art, has worked with me tirelessly to explore the museum's collection. Howard Dickinson is another photograph collector without whose knowledge I couldn't have managed.

Every photograph source in this endeavor has my thanks. They are mentioned at the end of each caption throughout the book.

My love and thanks go out to my husband, David, for keeping me fed and in clean clothes as I completed this project, and to my children, Matthew and Rachel, for understanding their mother's passion, as I talked about it nonstop.

Finally, I'd like to say a huge thank you to my editors, Liz Gurley and Maggie Bullwinkel, for presenting the project to me and for walking me through my first drafting and editing process.

INTRODUCTION

The area where the city of Douglasville sits is the highest point along the Tallapoosa Ridge, which runs east to west across western Georgia. At one time, not only was the area inhabited by members of the Cherokee Nation, but it was also inhabited by tribes making up the northern boundaries for the Lower Creek Nation.

Trouble began brewing for both tribes in 1802, when the State of Georgia entered into an agreement with the US government. Back then, the boundaries of Georgia went as far west as the Mississippi River. The US government sought control of the land, so it paid the State of Georgia $1.25 million, and in return, the State of Georgia returned control of its western lands back to the federal government. The US government promised to provide federal assistance in removing Native Americans residing in Georgia at a time later to be determined and as soon as it could be reasonably and peaceably done. For the next few years, Native American lands would be signed away via treaty, culminating in the final blow brought by the Trail of Tears.

By 1821, the two Native American nations had been fighting back and forth for several years. Tired of the constant fighting, the State of Georgia created a no-man's-land between the two tribes, beginning at Buzzard's Roost Island on the Chattahoochee River. It ran up through what is now Douglas County, along an old Indian trail heading northwest toward the Tallapoosa ridgeline. At some point, it crossed the Norfolk Southern railway track that exists today one mile east of midtown Douglasville, and then ran parallel with the track westward, past an old skint chestnut tree. Both tribes could enter the no-man's-land, but only to hunt and fish. The city of Douglasville sits within the no-man's-land today.

White settlers began to enter the area as early as 1820 to establish farms and communities. Carroll County was created in 1826, followed by Campbell County in 1828.

By 1831, Georgia surveyed the land and set out land lots. Enticed by wide-open land as well as the hint of gold, many white settlers flocked to Campbell County in the 1830s, including families with names such as James, Morris, Baggett, Winn, Weddington, Black, McLarty, Swofford, and Vansant, among many others.

They all traveled by wagon or horseback, crossing the Chattahoochee River and heading north up the trail. Along the way, they looked for a landmark they had heard about that would let them know they were heading the right way—a very tall tree. The story was passed along that the Native Americans who lived in the area had removed the bark off the tree to make it even more identifiable. The community that would spring up near the tree would also give it its name—Skint Chestnut.

Douglas County was created in 1870 from the section of Campbell County located on the north side of the Chattahoochee River. There was some disagreement regarding the location of the county seat. Some citizens wanted a location closer to the middle of the county, while others had their hearts set on Skint Chestnut. The Skint Chestnut folks continued on with plans while a lawsuit to settle the matter was pending.

It was only natural for the focal point of the town—the Douglas County Courthouse—to be built at the highest point along the Tallapoosa ridgeline. The first courthouse was built in 1871 as a temporary structure. Prior to this, there are stories that circulate that the first ordinary actually rented space in Young Vansant's store to conduct business.

Skint Chestnut became Douglasville when the act to incorporate the city was passed on February 25, 1875. The act called for an election to take place the first Saturday in March 1875 to elect a mayor, a recorder, and five aldermen. The election resulted in J.S. James as mayor, J.C. Pittman as recorder, and A.S. McCarley as marshal.

The second Douglas County Courthouse, constructed in 1880, was a two-story gray-brick building with eight rooms. There are no pictures of this structure, but eyewitness accounts have been handed down indicating that county offices were located on the ground floor, while the jury and witness rooms were on the second floor.

The second courthouse had to be demolished in 1884, as the building began to crumble away almost as soon as it was erected. Dated July 29, 1884, a grand jury report states, "We have made a thorough examination of the courthouse and find it in bad shape and perhaps in dangerous condition. We found large cracks in the walls and some key stones loose and apparently ready to drop out. We recommend that it be bolted and banded without delay." Improperly baked bricks and poor mortar were determined to be the cause.

During the 12 years it took to erect a new courthouse, county officials had to deal with a serious lack of funds in continuing to attempt to build a New South town from the ground up. Town fathers worked hard to add specific ingredients to meet the philosophy, including a cotton mill, the railroad, a hotel, banks, and a thriving commercial business district. Town fathers continually advertised the benefits of living and doing business in Douglasville. Newspapers of the day centered on cotton crops, church singings, and political news.

By July 1917, the men from Douglas County who were being drafted into service for World War I had their names on a list displayed at the Bartlett Building. The men left for service, while their families back home learned about rationing.

Douglasville experienced the Great Depression as early as 1927 with a major bank failure. Farmers suffered, and since merchants in town depended on the farmers' business, they suffered as well. Many stores closed their doors, including the cotton mill, which shut down for several months.

During World War II, the folks at home focused on war bonds. They did their part, with sales exceeding their set quotas each month. Many downtown businessmen trained for home-defense duty. Also during the 1940s, the cotton mill reopened, and Douglas County became the number-one grower of tomatoes in North Georgia.

The 1950s saw the beginning of a shift from agricultural pursuits to service-type businesses and manufacturing, and a new hospital and health center as well as the first public housing complexes were built.

Major growth was the focus during the 1960s, with Douglas County becoming more akin to a suburb as it joined the Atlanta Regional Planning Commission. From 1970 through 1980, Douglas County's population grew 86 percent. Much of the area's growth was concentrated near Interstate 20, which was completed through Douglasville in 1966. Shopping centers, fast-food restaurants, and small businesses sprang up along Highway 5 and Thornton Road, leaving downtown Douglasville behind.

Gradually, Douglasville did what it does best. It adjusted and reinvented itself to meet the needs of its citizens and visitors. Today, the downtown area is home to thriving restaurants, stores, and professional offices. A section of Price Avenue is now known as O'Neal Plaza, a pedestrian walk-through between Church and Broad Streets that hosts the Cultural Arts Center's Chili Cook-off each fall and the Taste of Douglasville each spring, along with live concerts. Douglasville also boasts a large convention center, which provides a venue for weddings, gala events, and monthly meetings.

One

FROM SKINT CHESTNUT
TO DOUGLASVILLE

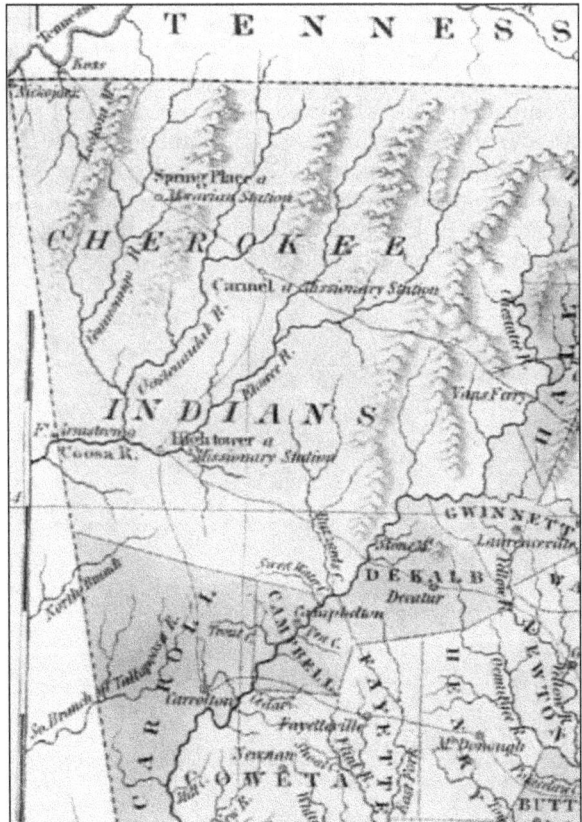

By 1835, droves of white settlers were pouring into the newly created Campbell County, including the Black family. Their claim included land on both sides of the Indian trail, at the highest point along the ridge, close to the old skint chestnut tree. Soon, Black saw the advantages of his location as more and more wagons passed his place. The story goes that he built a trading post, dug a well, and set up a few campsites for travelers to rest along their journey, all of which was referred to as Skint Chestnut. (Courtesy of Anthony Finley.)

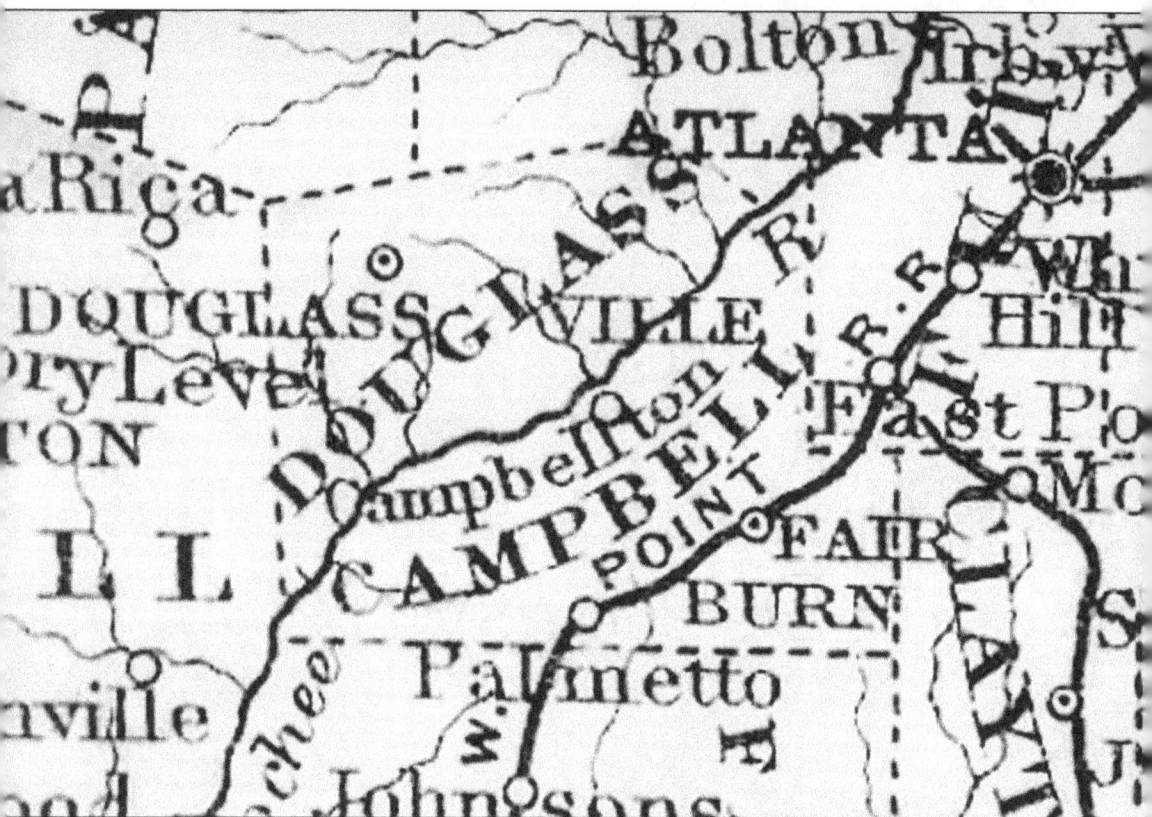

Eventually, people who lived on the north side of the Chattahoochee River grew tired of the two-day trip it took to travel the 20 miles to reach the county seat of Campbellton. A bill was prepared and introduced by Dr. W.S. Zellers, a representative from Campbellton, to create a new county on the north side of the river. The name of the new county would be Douglas in honor of Stephen A. Douglas, US senator from Illinois who ran against Abraham Lincoln in 1860. (Courtesy of Augustus Mitchell.)

The act that created Douglas County also named the first board of commissioners, including Ephraim Pray, the namesake for Pray Street on the west side of the Old Courthouse Museum. An election was held in November 1870 to choose other officials as well as the location of a county seat. Immediately following the election, Moses M. Smith, among others, filed an injunction, as votes that were not clearly for Skint Chestnut or Chapel Hill were put in the column for Skint Chestnut. The matter went all the way to the Supreme Court of Georgia before a second election was held in which voters finally settled on Skint Chestnut, which officially became Douglasville by legislative act on February 25, 1875. (Courtesy of the City of Douglasville.)

Young Vansant is remembered for donating 40 acres where the town site would be located at Skint Chestnut. The state historical marker in front of the old Douglas County Courthouse indicates both of the Vansant brothers—Young and Reuben—wanted to donate land for the new county seat. The marker indicates that the brothers had a "friendly fist duel" to decide which one would provide the land. Young Vansant won, and on January 9, 1871, he deeded 40 acres to the Douglas County Board of Commissioners within Lots 16 and 17 for the county site and public buildings. Vansant did make an exception in regard to the well that was on the property. Young Vansant is pictured here with his wife, Nancy. (Courtesy of the Douglas County Museum of Art and History.)

John M. Huey was hired as Douglas County's first surveyor, a position he would hold for 18 consecutive years. According to county historian Fannie Mae Davis, Huey created a map of Douglas County that, for many years, would be lauded by county attorneys as completely accurate. Huey later served in the state legislature from 1888 to 1889, during which he was described as the most methodical member of the general assembly. Over his lifetime, he accumulated several boxes of records from the various committees and groups on which he served. (Courtesy of Huey and Georgia McIntosh.)

Two

COURTHOUSE, RAILROAD, AND COTTON MILL

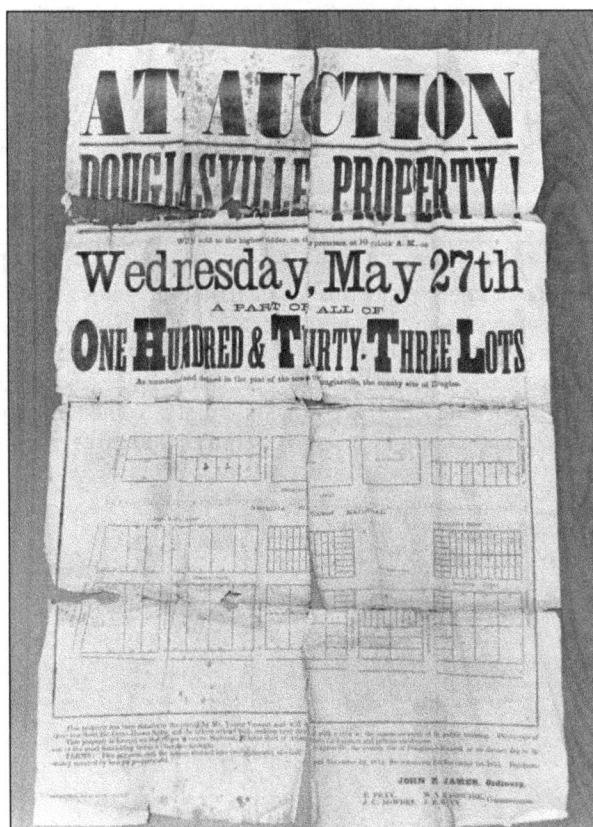

This handbill indicates some of John M. Huey's work as county surveyor. The blank square underneath the word "railroad" is the area where the old courthouse sits today, at 6754 Broad Street in downtown Douglasville. During March 1874, a notice ran in the Atlanta papers to encourage people to visit Douglasville and purchase lots. The terms of sale were five percent cash, with the balance to be paid in two installments—the first due in November 1874 and the remainder in November 1875. (Courtesy of Judge Robert James.)

Andrew J. Bryan & Company delivered this drawing to the Douglas County commissioners detailing the appearance of the finished courthouse. James Abercrombie furnished the pine for the floors and ceilings from the forests along the Dog River, while a company along the Chattahoochee River supplied the bricks. Thomas Franklin Brown was the brick mason, and T.C. Thompson & Brothers performed the construction, all at a contracted cost of $17,500. A grand jury report from 1897 indicates the courthouse clock, vaults, and furniture totaled $1,430.74. (Courtesy of the Douglas County Museum of History and Art.)

14

The main entrance and facade of the 1896 courthouse faced east, or Bowden Street. The two-story building had a 10-foot-wide hallway from end to end, with another hallway bisecting the main hall. Exterior doors were located at the end of each hallway. Rising from the building's slate roof was a four-faced clock tower that could be heard a mile away when it chimed the hour and half hour. (Courtesy of the Douglas County government.)

COURT HOUSE, DOUGLASVILLE, GA.

The tax collector/receiver offices were located under the northwest tower of the building. Also on the north side were the county commissioner, treasurer, and school superintendent offices, along with the clerk of superior court. (Courtesy of Judge Robert James.)

15

The ordinary's office was located along the southern side of the building. There was also an extra office that sources state attorneys would frequently rent. The justice of the peace and sheriff's offices were on the south side, too. (Courtesy of the City of Douglasville.)

The courtroom, two jury rooms, two witness rooms, and the solicitor general's office were located on the second floor. From 1911 to 1923, J.R. Hutcheson held the solicitor general's office for the Tallapoosa Judicial Circuit. (Courtesy of Phil Wren.)

The 1896 courthouse was completely destroyed by fire on January 11, 1956. The cause of the fire was attributed to faulty wiring in the basement furnace room. The fire broke out at 5:00 a.m., completely engulfing the building before the then-volunteer fire department could arrive. Communication broke down because the siren had suffered a short circuit. (Courtesy of Howard Dickinson's photocopy collection.)

By the time firefighters arrived on scene, the building was basically gone, so they turned their attention to keeping the fire away from surrounding buildings, such as the city hall, jail, First Baptist Church, and houses on Bowden Street, since high winds that morning made its spread a real possibility. Fire departments from Atlanta, Austell, and Villa Rica eventually arrived to assist as well. (Courtesy of Phil Wren.)

On June 6, 1956, a special election was held for a bond issue involving the construction of a new courthouse, which would be built in the international style with 52 rooms and several restrooms. The unique design appeared to be a single-story building from the front side, or Broad Street, but from the Church Street side of the building, the second story can be detected. Due to the terrain, both floors have entrances at ground level. Various materials were used in the construction, including glass, aluminum, glazed brick, polished granite, and North Georgia marble, among some black marble. Seen here from left to right are Douglas County commissioners Hugh Riley, H.L. Rawlins, and Arthur Meadows receiving the keys from builder Curtis McKown Sr. (Courtesy of the Douglas County government.)

In 1997, construction began on a new Douglas County Courthouse on Hospital Drive. The courthouse on Broad Street is now known as the Old Courthouse and is home to the Douglas County Museum of History and Art, as well as other community organizations. (Author's collection.)

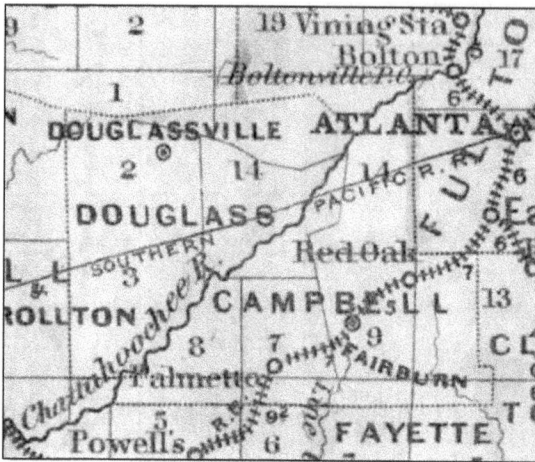

By 1870, the land had been cleared for the rail line from Atlanta to Skint Chestnut and beyond to Reuben Vansant's crossroads, near today's Bright Star Road. On July 12, 1873, a railroad meeting was held at Chapel Hill to discuss proposed routes and issues surrounding stock subscriptions. Three days later, a larger group met in Douglasville to consider the prospect of the Georgia Western Railroad passing through the county. A committee was formed to communicate with the railroad company, with W.P. Strickland as the chair and A.S. Gorman as secretary. (Courtesy of Asher & Adams.)

Railroad construction finally began eight years later, in 1881. By that time, the Georgia Western Railroad had become the Georgia Pacific, and fortunately, the final route included Douglasville. Track laying for the railroad began in November 1881, starting at the outskirts of Atlanta and moving in a westerly direction at the rate of one mile per day. Hundreds of people, many of whom had never seen a train, were on hand in April 1882 for the arrival of the first locomotive in Douglasville. Several women brought food for picnics, and horses were tied off a block or so away so the sound of the engines would not frighten them. (Courtesy of Howard Dickinson's photocopy collection.)

On May 10, 1882, the *Atlanta Constitution* announced the Georgia Pacific would begin a regular schedule to Douglasville. The original train depot was built in 1883 and existed until January 1899, when it was destroyed by fire. All was lost but a few bales of cotton that had been left on the dock. J.I. Oxford, the former pastor of the Baptist church, had moved to Atlanta the day before the fire, but he had all his furniture stored at the depot, waiting to be shipped east. Unfortunately, he was left with nothing. (Courtesy of Butch and Debbie Alley.)

The train connected Douglasville to Atlanta, to Birmingham, and to many other points beyond for travel and trade. William Jackson Stringfellow (left) and Franklin Stringfellow (right) are seen in the wagon. Those loading watermelons at the Douglasville depot in the early 1900s are unidentified. (Courtesy of Betty Ledbetter.)

Pictured is a steam engine pulling 46 freight cars through the S-curve on September 10, 1946. The S-curve is west of Douglasville, near the North Baggett Road crossing. Today, this is a popular spot for railroad photographers. (Courtesy of the Douglas County Public Library.)

A second depot was built almost immediately, serving Douglasville until 1916, when the third depot was built. Over the years, as the roads improved, trucks began carrying more freight and folks began to own more cars, so they became less dependent on the railroad. (Courtesy of Howard Dickinson's photocopy collection.)

According to Douglas County historian Fannie Mae Davis, a popular pastime for young people in Douglasville focused on the train. They would meet the No. 39 train each day as it headed west and watch as the mailbags were unloaded, as seen here in 1943. Dot Padgett is the woman at right, in the mail cart. Nell Holloway (left) and Muriel Fowler are standing with her. (Courtesy of the City of Douglasville.)

By 1952, there were 8 passenger trains and 10 freight trains passing through Douglasville each day. This is a pre-1956 view of Douglasville, looking west down the tracks. Up ahead on the right is the depot, and on the left is the beginning of the commercial district, with the courthouse clock tower visible high up on the ridge. (Courtesy of Howard Dickinson's photocopy collection.)

The last depot was closed in the 1970s, long after passenger service had been discontinued. In 1974, the building was auctioned off for $1 to the Sword family and moved to their Chapel Hill property, where it remains today. (Courtesy of Jeff Champion.)

OTTON MILLS.
GLASVILLE GA.

During Douglasville's earliest days, Church Street was known as Factory Street due to the city's very first cotton mill. Unfortunately, the Eden Park Mill was consumed by fire around midnight on April 7, 1895, and it was a total loss. Even though there was an entanglement of lawsuits and insurance issues to settle with the Eden Park fire, Joseph S. James and his partner, Simon Baer, began building a new mill, initially referred to as the Georgia Western Cotton Mill, half a mile east of the central business district. It was a better location, as it was parallel to the railroad and the 50-acre tract allowed for the construction of a mill village to house workers. (Courtesy of the City of Douglasville.)

GREAT ADVANTAGES RESULT

—FROM—

The PRARAY Improved System of Construction.

PATENTED APRIL 17, 1894.

Floors are Supported Independent of Walls.

Less Massive Brick Work required.

Lighter and Stronger in Construction, at a Less Cost of Erection.

A Less Fire Risk, consequently a Reduced Insurance.

THIRTY - THREE PER CENT. more light than can be obtained by any other system of construction.

33 PER CENT. less bricks in the walls.

10 PER CENT. less height of wall required.

10 PER CENT. less space to heat.

MEETS ALL POINTS REQUIRED by the Mutual Insurance Companies.

IS A SLOW BURNING CONSTRUCTION.

PRESENT EXAMPLES ERECTED ON THIS SYSTEM:

THE DIXIE COTTON MILLS, ... La Grange, Ga.
  Cost less per spindle for building than any mill built in the South. .

SELMA COTTON MILLS, ... Selma, Ala.

AFRO COTTON MILLS, ... ' . . . Anniston, Ga.

GEORGIA WESTERN COTTON MILL, . . . Douglasville, Ga.

THE THOMAS M. HOLT, } Thomas M. Holt Mfg. Co.,
THE ——— CORA ——— } Haw River, N. C.

SECTION THROUGH WALL AND WINDOW.

PLANS OF WALLS, ETC.
Patented by C. A. M. Praray April 17 1894

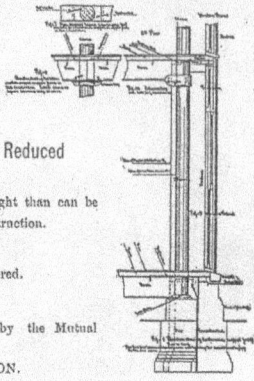

CORA COTTON MILL

WE PRINT below letters from Messrs. B. S. Robertson, Treurer of the Thomas M. Holt Mfg. Co., and of Samuel H Vice-President of the Dixie, and General Manager of Georgia Western Cotton Mills:

THE THOS. M. HOLT MANUFACTURING CO.

Haw River, N. C., April 4, 18

Messrs. Chas. A. M. Praray & Co., Providence, R. I.

Gentlemen:—Yours of the 2nd to hand. We should say that the lamps are lighted in the old of our mill 5 or 4 times as long during the day in the old part as they are in the new part. Of course, having weav the old part, and earding and spinning in the new part accounts for some of this, but even allowing for this, there a great difference in the matter of light in the new construction. We only wish we had the same construction part that contains the looms, since the light would be *decidedly* better.

We are fixing to put some looms in the Cora Mill this Summer, and we think the weave room there weminently satisfactory.

Yours truly,

(Signed) B. S. ROBERTSON, Treas

OFFICE OF THE GEORGIA WESTERN COTTON MILLS.

Douglasville, Ga., April 19, 18

Messrs. Chas. A. M. Praray & Co., Providence, R. I.

Gentlemen:—Your favor of the 10th duly received. In reply I beg to say that I have bui Cotton Mills in the South, using your "PRARAY" Patent Construction.

The Dixie Mills at La Grange, Ga., and the Georgia Western Cotton Mills of Douglasville, Ga. now construction, and nearly completed, and I am pleased to say that I am more than pleased with the plans and cor tion, and prefer them to any that I have seen for this class of buildings.

The Mills can be built cheaper with these plans, than with the ordinary mill construction, and are lighter and better adapted for the business in every way, being especially fitted to the Southern Climate.

It will give me great pleasure to give any of your friends or clients any further details, if they will come to Douglasville, Ga., or write.

Very truly yours,

(Signed) SAMUEL HALE, General Manager Georgia Western Cotton M

WE NAME YOU A FEW MILLS located in the Northern and Southern St of which Mr. Praray was the Architect and Constructing Engineer:

THE NORTHERN MILLS ARE:

The N. H. Slater, Webster, Mass.; Whitman Mills, New Bedford; The Corr Mills, Taunton, Two additions to the Whittin Bros., Mill at Whitinsville, Northbridge, Mass.; The River Sp Mills, Woonsocket, R. I.; The Vesta Knitting Mills, Providence, R. I.; The Kenyon Mi Shannock, R. I.

THE SOUTHERN MILLS ARE:

Two Mills for the Clifton Mfg. Co., Clifton, S. C.; Two Mills for the Anderson Cotton Mills, And S. C.; The Piedmont Mills, Piedmont, S. C.; The Pelham Mills, Pelham, S. C.; The Brones Brones, S. C.; The Raleigh Mills, Raleigh, N. C.; Tallassee Fall Mills, Tallassee Falls, Ala.; Aiken Bath, S. C.; Stonewall Mills, Stonewall, Miss.; The South Side Mills, Salem, S. C.; Caraleigh Raleigh, N. C., and many other smaller mills.

WATER POWERS

TWO FOR THE CLIFTON MILLS, CLIFTON, S. C.
ONE FOR THE TALLASSEE FALLS MFG. CO., TALLASSEE, GA.
ONE FOR THE PELHAM MILLS, PELHAM, S. C.
ONE FOR THE FRIES ELECTRIC AND POWER CO., SALEM, N. C.
TWO FOR THE CANADIEN COLORED COTTON MILL CO., CANA

On November 15, 1908, the *Atlanta Constitution* finally announced the Douglasville mill had begun operation the day before, 10 years after its initial proposal. By this time, the Geer family from South Carolina had partnered with Joseph S. James, and M.E. Geer had arrived in Douglasville to oversee its completion. The mill's name had also changed, becoming known as the New Century Cotton Mill. As far as cotton mills built during the New South time period go, the mill in Douglasville was very unique. It was only one of five mills built in the South using Charles Praray's innovative patent, under the name "Praray Improved Construction for Mills," and before it burned to the ground, it was only one of two where the telltale zigzag walls were still standing. (Courtesy of the City of Douglasville.)

OPPOSITE PAGE: When the Eden Park Mill was built, it lacked homes for the workers and their families. By choosing the mill site along Bankhead Highway and by having at least 50 acres, the company was able to build the mill village, which also included a company store, homes, and athletic fields, along with a pasture for any livestock workers might have. (Courtesy of the City of Douglasville.)

The cotton mill in Douglasville was an excellent example of the adaptation of northern architecture to the New South economy. The unique architecture of the mill, with two separate foundations, was a cost-saving device. The inner foundation housed the equipment, while the outer foundation and walls held the vast window casings. The walls were entirely free from strain, which allowed for more windows. Not only did this construction technique make it cheaper to build the walls, but also, in case of fire, they could be removed more easily and were less costly to replace. (Courtesy of the City of Douglasville.)

Not everyone who worked in the mill lived in the village, though. This is the Stringfellow boardinghouse on Strickland Street in the early 1900s. William Jackson Stringfellow (second row from top, third from right) not only took in boarders, he also owned a store near the mill where he sold groceries and dry goods. He was also the original owner of the space where the Palace Barber Shop was located for years, along with a cobbler shop next to Selman's Drugs, which is now the Irish Bred Pub. (Courtesy of Betty Ledbetter.)

Warner "Papa" Jackson and Nancy Ann Ragin moved to Douglasville in 1905 to work at the mill. They are pictured here with their six children, who are, from left to right, (first row) Myrtie, Andrew, and Bertha; (second row) Oscar, Homer, and Dollie. The couple would eventually have four more children, including the youngest, Claude, in 1917. (Courtesy of Derek Jackson.)

Jesse Lee Pepper and Maggie Lula Veal Pepper moved from Cleveland, Georgia, to find work at the mill in the mid- to late 1920s. Their property was located off Highway 92 and James Road in the Mount Carmel community. Maggie is buried at the Old Mount Carmel Cemetery. (Courtesy of Derek Jackson.)

Taken in 1910, this photograph shows Harold Ledbetter (left), his brother Douglas (center), and an unidentified child. Both of the young Ledbetters were taken out of school to work in the mill, where they had to stand on boxes to reach the looms in the spinning room. There were no child labor laws, and during hard times, everyone in the family had to pitch in to make ends meet. Workdays started at 6:00 a.m. and ended at 6:00 p.m. (Courtesy of Betty Ledbetter.)

There were many types of machines in the cotton mill, but this particular one is a ring-spinning apparatus, which dates back to the 1820s. Undergoing several improvements through the years, they required little physical strength and thus were manned by women and children. Doffers, usually young boys, would change out the spindles to keep the machines running. (Courtesy of Howard Dickinson's photocopy collection.)

The mill had a traveling baseball team, which was one of the best in the state of Georgia. Seen here is one of the Lois Cotton Mill baseball teams in the 1920s. Second from left, standing, is Raymond "Red" Ledbetter. Second from right, sitting, is Harold Ledbetter. (Courtesy of Betty Ledbetter.)

Guy Stringfellow played for the Lois Mill team around 1912. His father and uncle were city councilmen at the time the 1896 courthouse was constructed, as their names are imprinted in the cornerstone. (Courtesy of Betty Ledbetter.)

Betty Ledbetter was photographed in front of the old Clover Mill Village School in 1931 or 1932. In the late 1940s, the building underwent renovations and reopened as Douglas County's first hospital. Hundreds of Douglas County babies were born in this building, which still stands between Courtland Street and Senior Circle on Fairburn Road. (Courtesy of Betty Ledbetter.)

Adjacent to the mill was an office building, seen here in the 1940s. Folks who worked at the mill could use the recreation hall upstairs for Halloween parties in the fall and fish fries and barbecues in the summer. (Courtesy of the Douglas County Public Library.)

In the 1930s and 1940s, the mill was a major employer in Douglas County, making dresses and pants, in addition to two planing mills. The mill was involved in the Textile Worker's Strike of 1934, the largest labor strike in the history of the United States, with over 44,000 mill workers across Georgia on strike regarding various issues of discrimination and evictions. In the 1950s, the Glendale Mills purchased the mill for their parent company, J.F. Stifel. They ran three full shifts, six days a week, manufacturing broadcloth and printed fabric. During the 1970s and 1980s, the mill was known as the Desoto Mills and the Douglasville Spinners. (Courtesy of the Douglas County Public Library.)

As time went on, the building's appearance deceptively changed. At some point, the mill windows were taken out and bricked over, basically disguising its once unique features. The history and age of the building were mostly unknown due to its modern facade. The historic significance of the cotton mill was not noted until the 1990s, when the Georgia Department of Transportation (GDOT) conducted a survey of the impact area in correlation to the Highway 92 realignment project. In 1998, there was some discussion between Douglasville officials, members of the Georgia Trust for Historic Preservation, and GDOT employees regarding the mill and how it could be listed in the National Register of Historic Places due to its method of construction, but ultimately, the building sat ignored for a few more years. (Author's collection.)

The building that came to be abandoned and derelict as the 19th century moved into the 20th remained as such into the 21st century, until the early morning of May 12, 2012, when the structure became the victim of second-degree arson and burglary. Even though it was an early hour, dozens of Douglasville's citizens, such as these unidentified four, stood along the railroad tracks watching the mill burn. Eventually, the young men responsible were caught, tried, and sentenced to a probation detention center and community service. (Author's collection, via Stephanie.)

Three

CITY GOVERNMENT AND LAW ENFORCEMENT

Joseph S. James was elected as Douglasville's first mayor in 1875, and until his death in 1931, he remained an ardent Democrat who adhered to the New South philosophy. In addition to his land speculation and thriving law practice, James was instrumental in the construction of the cotton mill in Douglasville. He ran much of his empire from a brick building he had erected on the west corner of Bowden and Church Streets. At some point, he deeded the property to the city, with the stipulation that it must be used for municipal purposes. James deeded half of the lot to the city as a gift in 1911, while the other half, including the building, was deeded in 1922 for the price of $200. Referred to as the James Building, the structure was torn down in the 1930s. (Courtesy of the Douglas County Public Library.)

In 1916, under the administration of Mayor M.E. Geer, the city government of Douglasville moved from its single room in the Douglas County Courthouse, where city business had always been conducted, to an even smaller space directly behind the old R.M. Roberts Hardware Store at the corner of Campbellton and Broad Streets. The room was cramped and inadequate, but a lack of funds kept a new city hall from being built. (Courtesy of the Douglas County Public Library.)

In 1922, Douglasville's city council and mayor posed for a photograph. From left to right are (first row) Vander Smith, Jim Giles, Dr. T.R. Whitley, and Chester G. Brown, mayor; (second row) Gordon Banks, Glenn Dorris, Raymond Duncan, and Astor Merritt. (Courtesy of the City of Douglasville.)

In 1952, Mayor W.S. O'Neal flipped the switch at Southern Bell's new building on East Church Street, transferring Douglasville's telephone service from its former office above O'Neal's Drug Company to this new location. The need for an updated system indicated the tremendous growth the area had experienced since World War II. J.L. Whitney (left) and E.T. Blackman from Carrollton are also pictured. (Courtesy of the Douglas County Public Library.)

Under the administration of Mayor W.S. O'Neal, plans for a new city hall, located at the corner of Bowden and Church Streets, were announced at a citywide picnic in July 1952. The architecture firm of Peace & Smith designed modern spaces for the offices of the mayor and city clerk, the cashier's office and vault, and the police station, along with a room reserved for the new Douglas County Public Library. A council room was located on the second level, and in the rear of the building was the fire department. (Courtesy of the Douglas County government.)

The building at the corner of Church and Pray Streets housed the Rural Electric Administration (REA) and, later, Greystone Power. By the 1960s, Greystone moved to a new building on Bankhead Highway, at which time the REA/Greystone building became the Douglasville City Hall. The former city hall on Church Street that had been built under Mayor O'Neal's administration then became the home of the Douglasville Police Department. (Courtesy of the City of Douglasville.)

Members of the Douglasville City Council of 1961 are standing behind Mayor Jim Haddle and longtime city clerk Elma Shipp. Taking the job in the late 1930s, Shipp dealt with a potbellied stove as well as a 10-foot-wide oak desk that had been moved from the 1896 courthouse and used by each clerk. It sat higher than a normal desk, almost like a counter. The stove and desk followed Shipp through each reincarnation of the city hall until her retirement in the late 1960s. Standing are, from left to right, John Warren, Robert Alexander, Tom Worthan Sr., Jesse Pilgrim, Charlie Dodson, J.C. Arrington, and John Wynn. (Courtesy of the Douglas County Museum of History and Art.)

Douglasville City Council members of 1978 are, from left to right, (first row) Bob James, city attorney; Tom Worthan Sr., mayor; and John Wynn, mayor pro tem; (second row) Earl Albertson, Larry DeLoach, Charlie Camp, Rudolph Harper, Susan Cherry, and Homer Danley. (Courtesy of Judge Robert James.)

Charlie Camp began his career as a public servant when he became a city councilman in the mid-1970s, at which time Douglasville's population was a little over 5,000. As the 1990s rolled around, the projected population was somewhere between 14,000 and 15,000, resulting in issues related to traffic and parking in the downtown business district, including a study regarding the relocation of the railroad by a mile or two to the north. Mayor Camp was described as the only man in the world with a 24-hour-a-day part-time job. (Courtesy of Julie Camp.)

There are no photographs of what served as the Douglas County Jail prior to the 1890s, but in 1883, the grand jury detailed the jail as "unsafe, unhealthy and inconvenient." It recommended the ordinary sell the property and build another jail "where the jailor could reside within." During the term of Sheriff Fred Aderhold (1891–1892), Manley Manufacturing Company of Dalton constructed this building to serve as the county jail on Church Street. Sheriff Aderhold is seen at right on the second-floor balcony. (Courtesy of the City of Douglasville.)

OPPOSITE PAGE: In 1983, the sheriff's office and jail were moved farther west down Church Street to a new $3-million complex at the corner of Club and Church Streets. This administration center and jail provided better working conditions and equipment, which improved employee morale. Other benefits included self-sufficiency in feeding inmates and the ability to lodge prisoners from other jurisdictions. In 2013, under the leadership of Sheriff Phil Miller, the department moved to another new complex, on Fairburn Road. Fittingly, its access road was named for Douglas County's best-known sheriff, Earl Lee. (Courtesy of the Douglas County government.)

The 1890s jail was used through the administrations of 10 different sheriffs, with several modifications to the building over the years, including a remodel in 1954. The longest-serving sheriff was Alfred Seawright Baggett, who held office from 1911 through 1932. Upon election, he moved his family into the jail. The old jail site became a city parking lot and, recently, the home to the new covered parking deck next to the Douglasville Convention Center. (Courtesy the City of Douglasville.)

In the 1950s, Douglasville's four-man police force consisted of, from left to right, Clarence Pilgrim, J.C. Hicks, Walt McLarty, and Red Huckabee. According to then-mayor W.S. O'Neal, the brand-new police car was "one of the latest models geared for high speed when high speed was necessary." Built in the 1950s, the Douglasville City Hall is visible in the background. (Courtesy of the City of Douglasville.)

Four

HOSPITALS, CHURCHES, AND SCHOOLS

The first hospital in Douglas County emerged due to the efforts of Alma C. Gable. Weary of seeing so many mothers or their babies die during childbirth due to a lack of hospital care, Gable approached Douglas County commissioners in 1946 to form a hospital authority. Dr. W.S. O'Neal, Guy Baggett, William Chatham, R.H. Hutcheson, A.H. Stockmar, W.D. Palmer, E.M. Huffine, J. Cowan Whitley, and A.A. Fowler Sr. formed the first Douglas County Hospital Authority, choosing the old Clover Mills School on Fairburn Road to convert for hospital use. (Courtesy of the Douglas County government.)

The nurse standing at far left is Ruby Hembree, who not only worked as a nurse at the new Douglas County Memorial Hospital but also served as the hospital administrator for many years. Building the hospital was a community effort, with many citizens donating their time, labor, and materials. The facility opened in April 1948 with its first patient, five-year-old Richard Laird, who was in dire need of a tonsillectomy. (Courtesy of the Douglas County Museum of History and Art.)

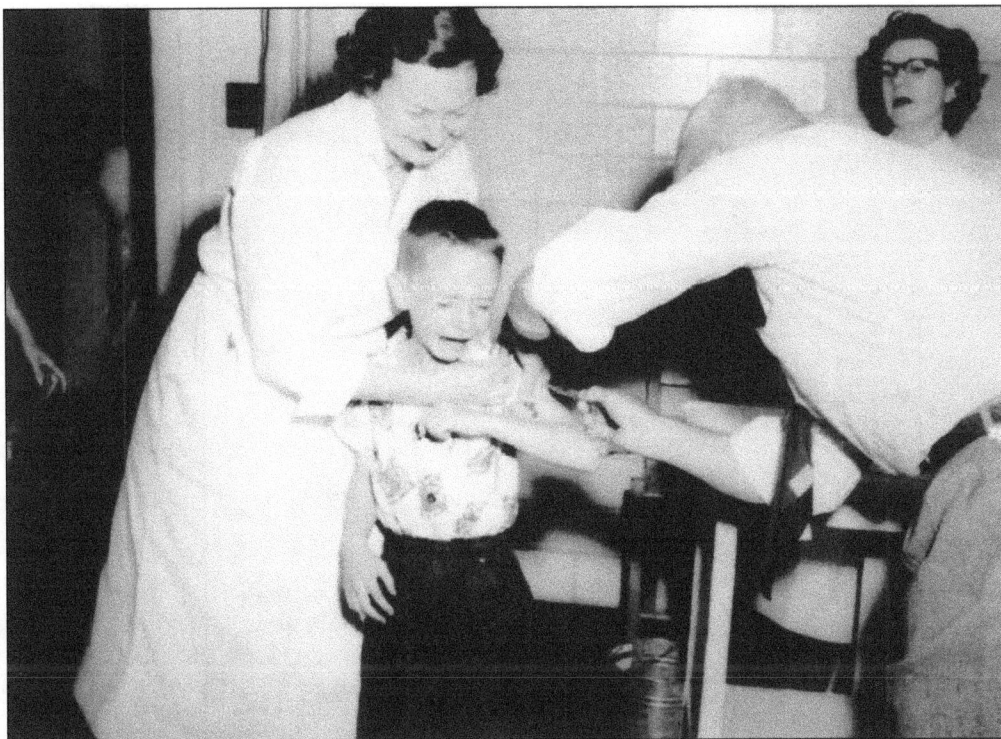

In the 1950s, a new health center was opened on Spring Street, behind the First Baptist Church of Douglasville. Many citizens can remember getting their school shots and sports physicals in this building before a new facility was built on Selman Drive. (Courtesy of Howard Dickinson's photocopy collection.)

Douglas General Hospital, located at Prestley Mill Road and Hospital Drive, began in 1974 with 15 doctors and 25 nurses. Now known as Wellstar Douglas Hospital, it has experienced tremendous growth over the years while still providing top-notch care for area citizens. (Courtesy of the Douglas County government.)

The exact date of the First United Methodist Church of Douglasville's organization is lost to history, but it is assumed to be as early as 1828, under the name of Flat Rock Methodist Episcopal Church. When Douglasville was created, the Flat Rock congregation decided to move to the new town. They tore down their church, salvaging some of the materials to erect a new building at the corner of Rose Avenue and Broad Street. Tremors from the Charleston Earthquake of 1886 dislodged the building from its foundation. Although repairs had been made to the structure, church members began searching for another location. Complete with stained glass windows, this building featuring medieval architecture was erected in 1889 at the corner of Church Street and Price Avenue. (Courtesy of Phil Wren.)

In 1921, a brick structure—complete with Sunday school rooms as well as a basement with an assembly room, kitchen, and small auditorium—replaced the wooden building. A larger auditorium/sanctuary would wait until 1941. In 1966, the church moved to its present location at 6167 Prestley Mill Road, and the building on Church Street was eventually removed. (Courtesy of the Douglas County government.)

BAPTIST CHURCH, DOUGLASVILLE, GA.

J. L. EELMAN & SON, PUBLISHERS

It is easy to remember the founding of the First Baptist Church of Douglasville, as it coincides with the establishment of Douglasville in 1875, when a lot was purchased on Church Street, across from the courthouse square. In April 1896, the church burned to the ground when the bell tower was struck by lightning. Members managed to save the church organ and pews, but the building was a total loss. This image dates to 1907 and represents the rebuilt church after the fire. At some point, a change had to be made to the main aisle and doorway to accommodate funerals. (Courtesy of Judge Robert James.)

The First Baptist Church that exists today is a result of a remodel to the sanctuary in the early 1940s, and in 1949, an education building added 35 classrooms to the growing church campus. In 1950, the church took on the official name of the First Baptist Church of Douglasville. This image is looking down Pray Street, to the west of courthouse square. (Courtesy of the Douglas County government.)

The Second Baptist Church of Douglasville, located at 4024 Highway 5, got its start in 1916 as the Mill Village Church on Bankhead Highway, east of the mill. (Courtesy of the Douglas County Public Library.)

Located at the corner of Spring and Campbellton Streets, the Spring Street School opened its doors in 1881. Later, it became the home of the Peace family. As president of the Civic League, Lola Peace began campaigns in 1914 to beautify the cemetery and build the pavilion located there today. The US Post Office also resides at this site. (Courtesy of Frankie Morris.)

The first public school in Douglasville was located at the corner of Chicago Avenue and Strickland Street. Built in the late 1870s, the school closed in 1888 when the Douglasville College opened. This structure still stands today but has been altered. (Courtesy of the Douglas County government.)

Spurred on by Dr. Thomas Whitley, the City of Douglasville finally saw the need to build the Douglasville College. Covering all grade levels, the school offered courses from needlepoint to Greek. The school opened in January 1889 at its location on Church Street, where the National Guard Armory stands today, and closed in 1914. (Courtesy of the Douglas County government.)

Here, Douglasville College students line up for graduation near the First Baptist Church. Graduation exercises generally lasted two to three days, with participation from all grade levels of the school. Programs would include speakers, skits, music, and recitations. (Courtesy of the Douglas County Museum of Art and History.)

Pictured is the Douglasville College class of 1901 on May 29, 1901. Third from left in the first row is Sally Kate Cooper, who went on to serve as a Methodist missionary in Korea for over 40 years. Next to her on the right is Faye Duncan. The only boy identified is Jerome Wilson, the last young man at right in the top row. (Courtesy of the City of Douglasville.)

This school was built in 1919 on the lot between the First Baptist Church and the National Guard Armory. The Douglasville Grammar School contained 25 classrooms, with anywhere between 600 to 800 students attending. Fortunately, when the brick-and-wooden building was lost to fire in 1955, there was no loss of life, as students and faculty had all gone home for the day. (Courtesy of the City of Douglasville.)

Still in existence today, student patrols at the Douglasville Grammar School began as part of a national program developed by the American Automobile Association, the Parent-Teacher Association, and the National Safety Council in the 1930s. In directing other students, not traffic, patrol members served as role models for their younger peers. (Courtesy of the City of Douglasville.)

Among those in Mrs. Jones's fifth grade class at Douglasville Grammar School in 1951–1952 were Jimmy Estes, Joyce Huey, Charlene Harper Popham, Nolan Shed, Charlotte Wright Carnes, Jane Ward Clarkson, Stuart Thompson, Barbara Horn, Carol Musser Nicholson, and Tommie Lou Hollis Moody. (Courtesy of Carol Musser Nicholson.)

Pictured here are members of the Douglasville Grammar School's faculty for the 1939–1940 school year. From left to right are Crystal Selman, Annie B. Morris, Ann Henderson Reeves, Bessie Frank McLarty, Geraldine Graves, unidentified, Florence Hutcheson, Mary Winn, Chester Kemp, Fain Boyd, Helen Huckeby, and Elsie Wood. (Courtesy of the City of Douglasville.)

This image of Douglas County High School was taken from the opposite side of Campbellton Street sometime during the 1950s. When voters decided a separate high school building was needed for students from across the county, ground was broken for the school on October 26, 1935, on the former home place of Dr. Tom Selman. (Courtesy of Huey and Georgia McIntosh.)

Members of the Future Farmers of America (FFA) can be seen working on a project behind the Vocational-Agriculture Building about 1940–1941. The FFA had helped to build the center, which was located on the Douglas County High School campus. The school's gymnasium is visible in the background. (Courtesy of the Douglas County Public Library.)

Pictured is a shop class with teacher Frank Cloer at Douglas County High School in the new Vocational-Agricultural Building in the 1950s. The building included a canning plant, blacksmithing shop, and woodworking shop, among other classrooms. (Courtesy of the Douglas County Public Library.)

Seen on Pray Street, with the courthouse to the left, the Douglas County High School marching band prepares for a parade in 1952. The First Baptist Church is visible across from the courthouse, with the Douglasville Grammar School at right. (Courtesy of the City of Douglasville.)

The Douglasville High School graduating class of 1928 includes, from left to right, (first row) Professor Adams, Tommye Feely, Raymond Walton, Nell Henry, Marvin Warwick, Ruth Meeks, William Maxwell, Edna Henly, Louis Burnett, Gladys Lee, Clonice Bomar, Marjorie Morris, and Guy Payne; (second row) Prof. H.J. Head; Eva Mae Waldrop; Mary Morris; Sara Brown; George Luther; Daisy Bomar; Wayne Giles; Elizabeth Wilson; Prof. H.R. Adams, superintendent; Inez Dorris, teacher; Gerald Humphries; Gladys Gilley; Robert Griggs; Kate Baggett; Pearl Gresham; and Will Thomas, teacher. (Courtesy of the City of Douglasville.)

The Douglasville High School football team is pictured here in 1934. From left to right are (first row) S.J. Wheat, Ralph Tuggle, Harold Mozley, K.B. Fincher, Hazzie Camp, Emmett Parish, and Belly Estes; (second row) James Baggett, Talmadge Wood, Charles Wilson, and Melvin Glover. (Courtesy of the City of Douglasville.)

Members of the FFA can be seen working on a project on the front lawn of the Douglas County High School, facing Campbellton Street. This image is unique in that it shows the homes that existed along Campbellton in 1941 and how rural the area was just a couple of blocks south of Broad Street. (Courtesy of the Douglas County Public Library.)

Coach Preston "Red" Camp (third row, far right) led the Douglas County High School's football squad of 1952. The Tigers ended up with a 4-6 record, losing two games in the last few minutes of play, including a match against Villa Rica. (Courtesy of the Douglas County Public Library.)

The Douglas County High School cheerleaders of the 1952–1953 school year are, clockwise from left to right, Barbara Godfrey, Bonnie Folds, Pat Haddle, Elaine Smith, Janice Browning, Jane Harding, Jo Ann Mason, Carole Dodd, and Pat McGouirk, many of whom still reside in the Douglasville area. (Courtesy of the City of Douglasville.)

Hutcheson High School, located at 6787 Forrest Avenue, is seen as it appeared in 1952, when Gertrude Hubert was principal. This building exists today as the Simpson & Daughters Mortuary. (Courtesy of the Douglas County Public Library.)

During the early 1950s, the entire city of Douglasville was involved with the Georgia Power Champion Home Town Contest, as seen with these Hutcheson High School students who are participating in a cleanup program of the grounds. (Courtesy of the Douglas County Public Library.)

Pictured is the pep squad of the 1955–1956 school year. From left to right are Isophene Harris, Joan Zachery, Mae Francis Moon, Velma Anderson, Louise Parker, Ida M. Pinkston, Ivylene Sharp, and Bernice Sharp. (Courtesy of Howard Dickinson's photocopy collection.)

The Hutcheson High School basketball team of the 1955–1956 school year includes, from left to right, Coach J.W. Stewart, Sammy Knight, Robert Crawford, Hasker Love, Robert Reid, Willie Smith, Charlie Arnold, Samuel Vance, Arthur Williams, Harold Springer, and John Etterson. (Courtesy of Howard Dickinson's photocopy collection.)

In 1952, Dorsey Denney, county agent, and Sheila Mashburn, club adviser, accompanied 23 members of the Douglas County 4-H Club on a trip to Camp Wahsega, near Dahlonega, for one week. Future Douglas County sheriff Tommy Waldrop gave a demonstration on livestock pest control, and Max Patterson of Lithia Springs participated in the junior public speaking program. (Courtesy of the Douglas County Public Library.)

The FFA Harvest Banquet was held in the gymnasium of the Douglas County High School in 1941. Dating back to 1929, the Future Farmers of America was a group of students, teachers, and agribusinesses that supported agricultural education as a testament to Douglas County's early agricultural roots. (Courtesy of the Douglas County Public Library.)

Irvin Meek, a Douglas County High School student, stands with his prize-winning mare. Meek served as the FFA treasurer, played on the basketball team, and won prizes at the local, county, and Macon state fairs. He received his Georgia planter degree in 1939. The Douglas County Courthouse is visible in the background. (Courtesy of the Douglas County Public Library.)

During the late 1930s and 1940s, the FFA of Douglas County High School was very active with various projects, such as this farm equipment demonstration on school grounds. (Courtesy of the Douglas County Public Library.)

With the motto "Learning to Do, Doing to Learn, Earning to Live, Living to Serve," the FFA played an important role in the lives of students, as a large majority of the county's population was involved in farming on various levels. In November 1940, members of the local FFA chapter, along with their sponsors, marched in the Armistice Day parade in Douglasville. (Courtesy of the Douglas County Public Library.)

Five

Downtown
Business District

This two-story brick building was one of the city's first permanent structures. In 1879, it housed the Dorsett, Price & McElreath General Store and Cotton Warehouse. In the 1890s, J.M. Roberts Hardware & Groceries was located here, as the photograph indicates, and during the 1930s, Hoke Bearden's store made this building home. Today, Precedence, Inc., is located there. (Courtesy of the City of Douglasville.)

This is a very early photograph of the intersection of Broad and Bowden Streets. In 1879, the building on the corner served as the offices of the *Weekly Star*, headed by Robert A. Massey. The editor was Charles O. Peavey, who was also the proprietor of a barbershop in the building. Later, this building was home to the Watson General Store, owned by John P. and Isaac M. Watson. The railway pedestrian bridge, constructed of cross ties, existed until the 1930s, when it was torn down. (Courtesy of Mike Garrett.)

OPPOSITE PAGE: In the 1880s, James A. Pittman constructed the two-story brick building seen third from left. Thomas A. Duke bought the building in 1886 to house his drugstore, until he died in 1902. Dr. T.R. Whitley moved his office here in 1903, and for a time, the post office was located here as well. From 1897 until 1909, Douglasville Lodge No. 289, F&AM, met on the second floor, which was destroyed by fire in November 1949. (Courtesy of the City of Douglasville.)

While the main focus of this photograph is the Douglasville Banking Company, the J.H. Selman home can be seen down the street, at left. Built in 1880, the home also served as an early hotel, located on the northwest corner of Price Avenue (today, O'Neal Plaza) and Church Street. Rooms were rented to traveling salesmen and railroad workers. Later, this was the first location of the Rural Electric Association (REA) and, even later, O'Neal's Clothing Store. Today, Douglasville's city hall sits on the spot. The Selman home was torn down in the 1930s to make way for the Alpha Theater. (Courtesy of the Douglas County government.)

G.G. Hudson and Dr. J.B. Edge constructed this building in 1885. After Hudson bought out Edge the following year, he sold the business to Joseph L. Selman (1855–1919), who studied medicine with Dr. W.H. Poole and graduated from the Atlanta Medical College. He was a well-respected surgeon in his day and opened his business, Douglasville's first drugstore, in 1885. It is the only building on Broad Street with distinctive cast-iron details. Today, the Irish Bred Pub calls this building home. (Courtesy of the City of Douglasville.)

Located at the corner of Strickland and Malone Streets, the Douglasville Hotel was built by Bose Adair of Atlanta in 1885. By 1909, it was known as the Perkins Hotel. Marion Morris was the last owner before it was torn down in 1938. (Courtesy of the City of Douglasville.)

In 1891, Lucious C. and Herschel M. Upshaw opened the Upshaw Brothers General Merchandise, Groceries, and Fertilizer store, where they built a thriving business. In 1909, their receipts totaled $100,000. Lucious served as a member of the city council in 1894, as state representative from 1909 to 1912, and as Douglasville's mayor from 1913 to 1914. Today, this space along Broad Street is home to Town and Country Upholstery. (Courtesy of the Douglas County government.)

The corner of Bowden and Broad Streets was once home to Vandiver's Dress Shop, as seen by the dress forms in the windows. The storefront immediately to the east was built before 1895 as a bank and then became the first home of the *Douglas County Sentinel* in 1902. Thomas R. Whitley, Lucious Upshaw, and James A. Pittman incorporated the paper, for which T.A. Majors served as the first editor. (Courtesy of the City of Douglasville.)

Beginning in 1885, N.B. and J.T. Duncan began moving inventory to the location that had been the original Skint Chestnut store before erecting their own building. In the 1870s, the same location had served as Douglasville's first saloon during the short-lived saloon era. Located at the corner of Pray and Broad Streets, the Duncan brothers' store was considered the largest mercantile business in West Georgia. It eventually took over the entire block, with a rail spur that crossed Bankhead Highway and went behind the store, where they provided a cotton buyers' yard and fertilizer shed. This photograph was taken in the late 1950s, when Thornton Chevrolet encompassed the western portion of the block. (Courtesy of Howard Dickinson's photocopy collection.)

Douglas Banking Company was doing business with the public as early as 1891 and moved into its new building at the northwest corner of Price Avenue and Church Street in 1906. The bank remained here until 1927, when it closed prior to the Great Depression. In August 1928, the First National Bank opened in the same location, with J.R. Hutcheson as president and Dr. W.S. O'Neal as vice president. Later, the bank became known as the Commercial Bank, now part of Regions Bank. This location has been home to other businesses, including Lee's Beauty Salon and, today, the Douglasville Welcome Center. Historians are unsure as to the event being celebrated in this picture. (Courtesy of the City of Douglasville.)

Douglas Hosiery Mill was located on the left side of Highway 92 North, across the railroad tracks. Originally, it was the home of Duntex Hosiery, which had a daily output of 19,200 socks. (Courtesy the City of Douglasville.)

Today, most people know this building on the northeast corner of Price Avenue and Church Street as the place where Dr. Clark Robinson, and until 2014 his daughter, Dr. Tammy Robinson, had their office, but originally, it was built in 1909 by the Douglasville Lodge No. 289, F&AM, along with Dr. J.R. McKoy and R.E. James. The lodge owned the second floor, while the post office occupied a portion of the first floor in 1914. The first floor held a variety of retail stores through the years, including Baggett's Pool Hall, a grocery store, and a shoe repair shop. In the 1940s, Dr. Ralph Hamilton and Dr. R.B. Turk had offices here. (Author's collection.)

In 1913, J.R. (Raymond) Duncan and P.D. Selman began selling Ford automobiles along Broad Street. According to the *Sentinel* advertisements from 1915, a Ford touring car could be bought for $530, while a roadster was $480. Notice the gas pump on the street. In 1985, this building became the offices of Hartley, Rowe & Fowler. (Courtesy of the City of Douglasville.)

To the right is the Banks Brothers General Store. In 1913, former teacher Jackson Monroe Banks built the brick store on Broad Street. By 1916, his brother J.B. Gordon Banks had joined him as a partner. (Courtesy of the City of Douglasville.)

In June 1914, V.R. (Vander) Smith closed the deal with J.T. Duncan for the two lots just west of the Douglasville Banking Company, along Broad Street. According to the *Sentinel*, Smith intended to build a movie theater known as the Crescent Theater with "an attractive ticket booth, mahogany woodwork and a performance stage." The theater was sometimes referred to as the Kozytorium. Smith also made a living as a cotton buyer and fertilizer dealer, in addition to his involvement with local politics. By 1918, he was the mayor of Douglasville. The theater remained open through the late 1920s. Today, Fabiano's Pizza occupies the space. (Courtesy of the City of Douglasville.)

Opened in 1915, Mozley Grocery on Broad Street (next door to today's Hartley, Rowe & Fowler) gained a reputation over the years for its fine meat department. Housewives could place their order by phone, and a deliveryman would bring it right to their kitchen table. Originally owned by Sam and Nat Mozley, the business changed hands a couple of times before finally closing in the 1980s. (Courtesy of the City of Douglasville.)

Constructed by Judge Robert H. Hutcheson in 1915, the Hutcheson Building on Broad Street is one of two buildings with the original owner's name still emblazoned on its facade. Hutcheson placed his law firm and other offices on the second floor, while the US Post Office took over the entire main floor, a testament to how fast Douglasville was growing. The smaller door to the right contained the stairwell that led to Hutcheson's offices. Other businesses located in the Hutcheson Building have included Hoke Bearden's Store in the 1930s. Today, the building is home to the very popular Gumbeaux's Cajun Café. (Courtesy of the City of Douglasville.)

Joseph C. McCarley's building on Broad Street is the other structure that boasts the name of the owner/builder as part of its design. McCarley started his business in a wooden structure before building this brick storefront in 1915. (Courtesy of the Douglas County government.)

J.C. McCarley did what it took to make his novelty store profitable. Here, McCarley is selling peanuts on the street, and in a *Sentinel* advertisement from 1919, he featured a Kodak camera for $2. In a few years, Ray's Café and Lamar's would be located in this spot, and today, it is home to Magnolia One Realty. (Courtesy of the City of Douglasville.)

Located at the east corner of Campbellton and Broad Streets, the Farmers & Merchants Bank opened in 1907 as part of the Witham Bank chain. The round window above the door and the fan windows along the sides of the building both contain German glass. (Courtesy of the City of Douglasville.)

In 1922, the Farmers & Merchants Bank was decorated for the Fourth of July. Chester G. Brown is visible in the window. By 1927, the bank had gone out of business, but through the years, its location has been home to numerous establishments, including Powell's Grocery and Douglasville Printing Company. (Courtesy of the Douglas County Museum of History and Art.)

In 1905, J. Walter House opened his cotton gin on the west side of Broad Street, where he had six cotton gins running simultaneously during the picking season each year. He also had a planing mill, and by the time this picture was taken in the 1920s, House was producing 10 tons of ice a day to supply the needs of citizens. (Courtesy of the City of Douglasville.)

Eventually, House's sons, W. Lawrence and Floyd, joined him, and the business became known as J.W. House & Sons. A few years later, his sons would operate the Douglasville Cement Company at the same location. (Courtesy of the City of Douglasville.)

Alpha A. Fowler Sr. first screened movies in the old Crescent Theater on Broad Street before opening the Alpha Theater on Price Avenue in the 1930s. The building burned soon after but was rebuilt. Today, Douglasville's city hall is located there, and this section of Price Avenue is known as O'Neal Plaza. (Courtesy of the City of Douglasville.)

Taken from the vantage point of the southeast corner of Price Avenue, looking north, this photograph shows the Alpha Theater. Local children visited the theater to take advantage of the double features. Many sat through the movies twice, which meant they were at the Alpha from 1:00 p.m. until 9:30 p.m. Today, this portion of Price Avenue is O'Neal Plaza, and the entrance to Douglasville City Hall is where the theater was located. (Courtesy of Huey and Georgia McIntosh.)

B.R. Kirkley was destined to be in the automobile business when he began working for the J.R. Duncan Motor Company in 1919. Later, he worked for himself, selling cars from his yard, and by 1930, he had become the Chevrolet dealer for the city of Douglasville. He located his business on West Broad Street, where it remained until he died in 1954. Kirkley was known for his community spirit, furnishing cars for parades and scholarships for students. (Courtesy of the City of Douglasville.)

Locals knew Bert Stone's Place as Stone City, located two miles east of Douglasville on US 78/ Bankhead Highway. The gentleman sitting in the chair out front has been identified as Bert. (Courtesy of Huey and Georgia McIntosh.)

Many travelers knew the home of A.W. and Ossie McLarty as the Old South Tourist Home, located at the corner of Church Street and Price Avenue. The property was sold in September 1959 for the construction of the Trust Company Bank of Douglas County. Today, the lot is home to the Douglasville Convention and Visitor's Center. (Courtesy of the City of Douglasville.)

At one time, there were three taxi companies operating in Douglasville. The three vehicles seen here in the mid-1950s were part of the City Cab Company. From left to right are Mr. Lee, E.C. New, and Ira Mason. The bus station was also located at this corner prior to its home on Adair Street. (Courtesy of the Douglas County Public Library.)

For many years, Southern Motor Lines had its stop at the corner of Broad and Campbellton Streets, but it eventually moved to a permanent home at Bankhead Highway and Adair Street. Mrs. Ira Mason managed the station. Later, the building would become Godfrey Insurance. (Courtesy of the Douglas County government.)

Originally, this dealership was located across the tracks on Broad Street at the Pure service station, but it made a new home on the corner of East Strickland and McCarley Streets. Today, this location is home to Mitchell Appliance. (Courtesy of Phil Wren.)

In the early 1950s, A.W. Thomas (of the Thomas Furniture Company) from Bainbridge purchased the old hosiery mill across the tracks on Highway 92 to open a furniture factory. Many Douglas County citizens took jobs there as upholsters and woodworkers. (Courtesy of the Douglas County Public Library.)

The Confederate Inn was located at the corner of Pray and Broad Streets. Marvin Hunt opened this restaurant, with private dining rooms, on April 19, 1952. At that time, a T-bone steak with french fries and a salad cost only $2.50. (Courtesy of the Douglas County Public Library.)

The Lucky Star Café was located at 6378 East Broad Street and was operated by Marvin Hunt. Later, this was the location of the Johnny Morris Tire Company. (Courtesy of Howard Dickinson's photocopy collection.)

In this scene looking west down Bankhead Highway and the railroad, midway down the first block of downtown buildings, homes can be seen along Strickland Street, Douglasville Banking Company can be seen at the corner of Bankhead Highway and Price Avenue, and the courthouse clock tower can be seen in the distance. FFA members created rock curbing financed by the City of Douglasville to create a barrier for cars between the highway and the railroad. The Junior Women's Club also participated in the project, planting small trees and shrubs. (Courtesy of the Douglas County Public Library.)

City leaders look over improvements to the city water works in the late 1940s. From left to right are (seated) Arthur King, businessman; Elma Ship, city clerk; and Harold Mozley, mayor; (standing) P.D. Mathews, publisher of the *Sentinel*; J.C. Arrington, superintendent of the water department; T.P. Huckaby, councilman; Comer Teal, policeman; and J.W. McClarty, policeman. (Courtesy of the City of Douglasville.)

This photograph of Thornton Chevrolet employees was taken in 1957, soon after the business took over the former Kirkley Chevrolet space on Broad Street. Among those in the image are Carlton Boyd, Bill Thornton, Ray Wright, Jane Jordan Pilgrim, Kate Baggett, C.L. Turner, Bill Calloway, Joe Reagan, Marvin Deal, Bill Gray, Tom Wisdom, R. Wilkins, Jimmy Huey, Bobby Stallings, Earl Carden, W.D. McLarty, Hoyt Rayburn, Bill Connally, Calwin Seymore, and T.W. Connally. (Courtesy of the City of Douglasville.)

George Edward Shell (second from left) is standing in front of his Amoco station at the corner of Fairburn Road and US 78/Bankhead Highway. The other men are unidentified representatives of Amoco. (Courtesy of the Douglas County government.)

Starting out as Powell's Grocery, this business was located in the old Farmers & Merchants Bank building at the southeast corner of Broad and Campbellton Streets. Later, Nick and Sara Nell Nicholson changed its name to The Store and relocated it to their own building, farther back on the west side of Campbellton Street. The building is still there today, in the Regions Bank parking lot. (Courtesy of Carol Musser Nicholson.)

Just like Mozley's Groceries, Powell's/ The Store offered home delivery, which meant Sarah Nell Nicholson spent most of her day on the phone taking orders. When the Nicholsons sold the bank building, Douglasville Printing took over the space, where it would remain for quite a few years. (Courtesy of Carol Musser Nicholson.)

Pictured is Red Barn Antiques, which was owned by Bill Wilson from the late 1950s through the 1960s. Wilson would stock his store, located on Bankhead Highway west of town, with antiques, gifts, and railroad salvage. His stock was constantly changing, and that's what brought people back time after time. (Courtesy of the City of Douglasville.)

Heading east on Church Street, the rear of Brumbelow Plumbing can be seen under construction, with the McElreath house next door. Across Church Street, the front doors of Baggett Hardware are also visible. Today, Uptown Dental is located in the Brumbelow Plumbing space. (Courtesy of Judge Robert James.)

In the 1950s, a group of citizens decided the vacant lot beside the Alpha Theater on Price Avenue needed a little park—a place for children to play. This view shows the northwest corner of Price Avenue and Church Street, where O'Neal Plaza sits today. The City of Douglasville took over the Alpha Theater's spot in 1995. (Courtesy of the Douglas County Public Library.)

A view up Broad Street in the 1950s shows a great sign of the times, a cute little unidentified young lady, and parking meters the City of Douglasville had installed for a while. Citizens complained bitterly, and they were eventually removed. (Courtesy of Howard Dickinson's photocopy collection.)

Owned by M.J. Morris, Douglasville Dry Cleaners, seen here at its Church Street location, changed venues a number of times over several years. Morris got into the dry cleaning business when he took his own pants to a store and decided he could do a better job of running the business. (Courtesy of the Douglas County government.)

M.J. Morris of Douglasville Dry Cleaners is shown standing next to one of his washing machines. Morris never took vacations but would visit as many antique stores as possible to add to his collection of historic irons and washing equipment. Today, his collection is on display at the Douglas County Museum of History and Art. (Courtesy of the Douglas County Museum of History and Art.)

Paul Cochran, pictured in 1967, was a longtime employee of Douglasville Dry Cleaners who handled the pickups and delivery. Everyone was familiar with his delivery van, which had the words "Here comes Paul!" emblazoned on the side. He was trusted to come and go at every home, even when the owners were not there. Folks would find their dry-cleaned garments lying neatly on their beds. (Courtesy of Frankie Morris.)

Originally known as Cracker Asphalt, the Young Refining Company was founded by Dr. C.B.F. Young in the 1950s, when the Bankhead Highway property was still surrounded by cornfields. The name "Cracker" referred to the cracking process that occurs when refining petroleum. (Courtesy of Howard Dickinson's photocopy collection.)

Originally, the corner of Price Avenue and Broad Street was the location of M.M. Smith's law office. J.B. Edge opened a drugstore there on New Year's Day 1885, followed by J.L. Selman's drugstore, which was sold to Dr. W.S. O'Neal in 1926. Later, it was known as the B&W Drugstore. Susanne Hudson had an antique store here before the space became the Irish Bred Pub. (Courtesy of the City of Douglasville.)

Since Douglasville's earliest days, there has been one mule barn or another located at different spots around town, under the control of one Abercrombie family member or another. The Abercrombie mule barn was known far and wide for fair deals for livestock and feed. In 1915, Joe S. Abercrombie was handling 250 head of mules at $50,000 annually. The Abercrombie family was also involved with the Farmers & Merchants Bank, with Joe S. Abercrombie serving as a stockholder and his brother Claude as president. Mac Abercrombie would be elected as sheriff in 1932, a position he held for 20 years. In the 1960s, Claude Abercrombie would also serve as sheriff. (Courtesy of Howard Dickinson's photocopy collection.)

OPPOSITE PAGE: R.L. Smith, a Douglasville businessman, held political office as chairman of the Douglas County Board of Commissioners. Around Christmas 1960, this photograph was used in a newspaper advertisement for his Economy Auto retail store. (Courtesy of Bob Smith.)

Through the 1950s, it was common to walk out of the Douglas County Courthouse and see mules and other animals on Bowden Street, as the Abercrombie Mule Barn was located at the corner of Church and Bowden Streets. (Courtesy of the Douglas County Public Library.)

Dr. T.R. Whitley's son operated the J. Cowan Whitley Funeral Home at this location west of town on Broad Street for many years. Later, the business became known as the Whitley-Garner Funeral Home. When it moved to its new location on Rose Avenue, Hightower Memorial Chapel took over the space. (Courtesy of Howard Dickinson's photocopy collection.)

For many years, this blacksmith shop was located on Church Street, next to the Huffine warehouse building. When it was torn down in 1953, R.J. Banks built a new brick building, which still stands today. W.C. McLarty's farm supply and hardware business would later open there. (Courtesy of the Douglas County Museum of History and Art.)

Six

PEOPLE, HOMES, AND EVENTS

Today, the residents of Douglasville recognize the Roberts-Mozley house as the home of the Cultural Arts Council of Douglasville & Douglas County, located at 8652 Campbellton Street. In 1901, W.T. Roberts and his wife, Emma Quillian Roberts, built the home, which was well appointed for the time period, with pocket doors, stained glass, and tiled fireplaces throughout. An interesting courting bench is located by the front door. (Courtesy of the Douglas County Museum of History and Art.)

As one of the first attorneys in Douglasville, W.T. Roberts was very involved with various events. He read the Declaration of Independence at the city's first Fourth of July celebration in 1886 and addressed Confederate veterans when Douglasville hosted the 7th Regiment's reunion in 1901. Roberts also served as mayor of Douglasville in 1884 and as a state representative in 1911. (Courtesy of the City of Douglasville.)

The W.T. Roberts family is pictured sitting on the front steps of their home on Campbellton Street around 1911. From left to right are (first row) Beryl, Will, Coral, two unidentified women, and John; (second row) an unidentified woman in a rocking chair and Osgood; (third row) an unidentified woman and man, Emma Q. Roberts, and Judge W.T. Roberts. When he received a government appointment in 1914, W.T. Roberts sold the house and moved his family to Washington, DC. (Courtesy of the City of Douglasville.)

T.N. Mozley, an owner of Mozley Groceries on Broad Street, bought the Roberts home in the 1920s. He served as mayor of Douglasville in 1936, and 10 years later, his son Harold would also be elected mayor. (Courtesy of the City of Douglasville.)

Douglas County celebrated its 50th birthday in 1945 with a Diamond Jubilee celebration. As grand marshal, Harold Mozley (son of T.N. Mozley) led the parade down Broad Street by riding a Brahma bull. Following his naval career, Harold was elected as mayor of Douglasville, taking office in January 1946. Mozley's time in office attracted some state and national news coverage since, at age 28, he was one of the youngest people in the country to be serving as mayor. (Courtesy of the City of Douglasville.)

Today, the Hutcheson home, located on Campbellton Street, is known for its beautiful gardens and attention to authentic detail, all of which are due to current owner Susanne Hudson. The home was built by J.R. (James Robert) Hutcheson, an 1894 graduate of Douglasville College. The property's other claim to fame is Judge Hutcheson's grandchild Susan, who cowrote the song "I Love the Nightlife" with Alicia Bridges in this house in 1977. (Courtesy of the Douglas County government.)

J.R. Hutcheson also served as solicitor general for the Tallapoosa Judicial Circuit from 1911 to 1923 and as judge for the Tallapoosa Judicial Circuit from 1933 to 1939. Before integration in the 1960s, one of Douglasville's colored schools was named for Judge Hutcheson. After teaching for a time, Hutcheson earned a law degree and entered practice in Douglasville with fellow attorney and mentor W.T. Roberts. Hutcheson was elected mayor for three different terms, during which time he was instrumental in leading the City of Douglasville as it built a power plant in 1909. (Courtesy of the Douglas County government.)

Built by Dr. F.M. Stewart and his wife, the former Willie Edna Selman, this home on Church Street still stands today, though it is missing its wide wraparound porch. Dr. and Mrs. Stewart raised six children in this home. Beloved by many, they were referred to as "Doc and Miss Willie." (Courtesy of the City of Douglasville.)

Dr. Stewart, seen here, and his older brother, Rader (Eldorado R.), became fixtures in the Douglasville business community in the 1890s. In addition to his thriving dental practice, Dr. Stewart was a member of the Masonic lodge, the Methodist church, and the school board. The brothers also owned several farms together and were investors in the Farmers & Merchants Bank. (Courtesy of the City of Douglasville.)

J.B.C. (John Bolton Chapel) Quillian, better known as Pastor Quillian, was a circuit-riding Methodist minister as early as the 1840s. When he retired from the circuit in 1875, he moved his family to Douglasville, where he and his wife, the former Elizabeth Causey, built this American Gothic home on Campbellton Street in the early 1880s. The home features a winding staircase and mahogany handrails and balusters. (Author's collection.)

In retirement, Reverend Quillian served as one of the first pastors of the First Methodist Church and wrote features and poetry that were published in the *Weekly Star* newspaper. He also wrote two books, titled *The Golden Lamp* and *Star of Redemption*. (Courtesy of the Douglas County Museum of History and Art.)

Capt. Caleb P. Bowen and his family are pictured on the steps of their home, located on West Broad Street, around 1900. Captain Bowen, his wife Melissa, and their granddaughter Annie Mary are seated on the lower step. Bowen earned the title of captain during the Civil War, when he served with the Campbell County Sharpshooters. Bowen was one of Douglasville's earliest politicians, serving as the first Douglas County treasurer in 1870 and as a state representative in 1876. To celebrate Pres. Grover Cleveland's election in 1884, Captain Bowen rode a mule up Broad Street. (Courtesy of the Douglas County Public Library.)

The Canning Center, which opened during the summer of 1941, was located in the rear of the Vocational-Agriculture Building on the Douglas County High School campus. Citizens were encouraged to can their own fruits and vegetables and stock up for the lean years ahead, as the government was buying up canned food for the Army. Under the supervision of C. Fred Ingram, the center was part of the vocational defense program, operated three days a week. (Courtesy of the Douglas County Public Library.)

John Brown Gordon Banks (1885–1966) spent a few years teaching before serving as a member of Douglas County's school board, during which time he was instrumental in the construction of the Douglas County High School. Banks also spent a total of 15 years serving as a member of the Douglasville City Council and at least 50 years as a partner, with his brother J.M. (Jack) Banks, in Banks Brothers, a Broad Street mercantile business. (Courtesy of the City of Douglasville.)

This home on Price Avenue began as a three-room cottage, built by Judge Robert A. Massey for his bride, Sara Emma McElreath, and her son, Glen (from a previous marriage), in 1878. In addition to Massey, the Selman family once owned the home, and today, it is owned by Douglas County historian Dot Padgett. (Courtesy of the Douglas County government.)

Known as the Poole-Huffine-Bulloch-Rollins-Hudson/Farmer-Rollins home, this Federal-style mansion was built by W.H. (William Haynes) Poole, the very first physician and surgeon in the area before Douglasville or Douglas County existed by name. Dr. Poole was very well known in town and took part in many aspects of the development of Douglasville. Constructed with wooden pegs, the home boasts an original slate roof. After spending a few years as a wedding and event facility, the home is once again a private residence. (Courtesy of the City of Douglasville.)

Though he was born in North Carolina, E.M. (Eugene McCullough) Huffine often visited Douglasville as a route salesman for the Robeson Company out of New York City. In fact, he met his future wife, Lizzie Dorris, at the Douglasville depot. Huffine gave up his sales job and opened a cotton warehouse and fertilizer business on Church Street. In the 1930s, he and his wife bought the Poole mansion on Strickland Street, where they raised their family. Huffine was also involved in county and city affairs, serving as one of the founding directors of the First National Bank in 1928 and as a member of the very first Hospital Authority board in 1946. (Courtesy of the City of Douglasville.)

J.A. (Joseph Alonzo) Huey served the county for over 25 years as a mail carrier. He began his job as one of two RFD postal carriers for Douglas County once the community system was abolished in 1902. Huey is seen here with his wife, Abbie, and their children, Huey and Helen, at their home on Huey Road. From left to right are (first row) Joseph and Abbie Huey with Huey and Helen; (second row) Bob Huey and Ellie and Fred Huey with Fredda; (third row) Louise McIntosh, Eula Huey, and Frank Huey; (fourth row) Mattie Lewis, Ernest McIntosh, Mary Huey, Nettie Huey, and Steve Huey. (Courtesy of Huey McIntosh.)

Joseph S. James and his wife, Margaret Elizabeth Maxwell, had five children. Sadly, their two boys died extremely young. In fact, one of the sons was the first burial at Douglasville's City Cemetery on Rose Avenue. Their daughters are seen here: (from left to right) Eunice (1882–1931), who died the same year as her father; Odessa (1872–1900), who married Rader Stewart shortly before her death; and Lois Cleveland James (1884–1906), who the cotton mill was named for at one point. (Courtesy of the Douglas County Museum of History and Art.)

C.C. Post and his wife, Helen Wilmans Post, were the original owners of this Chicago Avenue home. After moving to Douglasville in 1885, C.C. caused a major division in the local Democratic Party due to his involvement with the Populist Party, and Helen operated a mail-order faith-healing business. Within a few years, they were run out of town. Joseph S. James bought the house, where he would remain at the turn of the century. Later, it became a nursing home before being torn down. (Courtesy of the Douglas County Museum of History and Art.)

This photograph was taken when the Douglasville Post Office (now Gumbeaux's Cajun Café) took up the entire first floor of the Hutcheson Building. Frank Winn is the dapper gentleman in the straw hat. Winn is remembered as a long-serving court official, as he inherited his father's unexpired term for Douglas County clerk of court in 1915. During the following term, he assumed the role of deputy clerk. He held that position for the next 11 years, and after a break, he served again from 1946 to 1948, at which time he was elected to the clerk's position, which he held until 1965. Winn is also remembered as a consummate historian of Douglas County. (Courtesy of the City of Douglasville.)

The M.E. Geer home still stands at the corner of Colquitt and Strickland Streets. It was built in 1907, when Geer was superintendent of the cotton mill. The home is distinctive in that the granite foundation stones and front steps were carved from the retaining pond on the cotton mill property. Geer went on to serve a term as mayor in 1916. (Author's collection.)

Astor Merritt, an attorney, served as Douglasville's mayor for two terms, 1928–1929 and 1940–1941. He also held a post with the state attorney's office during the 1940s. This 1896 photograph was taken in his office in the courthouse. (Courtesy of Phil Wren.)

This is a northerly view of Bowden Street, looking toward the home where brothers Frank C. and Nick Winn now have their law practice. This photograph might date to February 1942, when 24 inches of snow accumulated in the city of Douglasville. (Courtesy of Howard Dickinson's photocopy collection.)

Douglas Bowl, located east of town on Bankhead Highway, advertised "top-notch lanes with equipment in peak condition and a snack bar for your pleasure," as well as billiard tables. Many folks bowled here in the 1960s and 1970s. From left to right are Kate Baggett, Mary Nell Entrekin, Polly ?, and Louise Hayes Thompson. (Courtesy of Mike Garrett.)

Around 1890, Confederate veteran James A. Dickinson and his wife, Martha, moved to the Crumbies District of Douglas County, where they raised seven children who have many living descendants throughout the county. (Both, courtesy of Howard Dickinson's photocopy collection.)

In 1952, Douglasville built its first housing project, which was segregated due to the times. The Chicago Avenue homes were for whites, while the Canzadie Keith homes were for blacks. Members of the Housing Authority were J.M. Haddle, Lamar Smith, R.L. Lloyd, A.A. Fowler Jr., and W.S. O'Neal. (Courtesy of the Douglas County Public Library.)

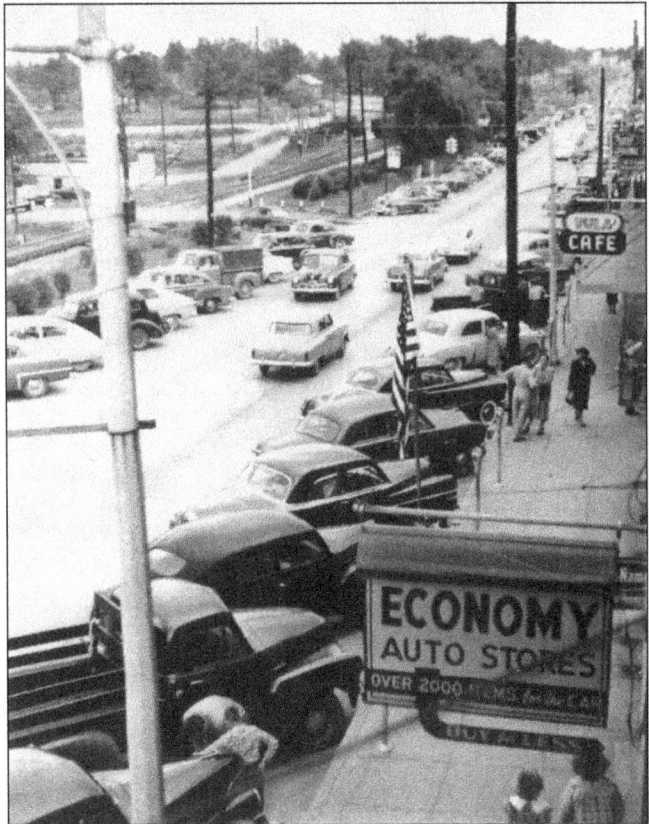

Local historians believe this image was taken from an upstairs window of the Hutcheson Building on Broad Street in 1952, when photographer Quillian Bonds had his studio there and Economy Auto was located on the ground floor. (Courtesy of Howard Dickinson's photocopy collection.)

The Evan R. Whitley family poses for the camera in the 1890s. Whitley served as Douglas County's second sheriff in the mid- to late 1870s. His son Dr. Thomas Rice Whitley (second row, center) served in the state legislature, founded Douglasville College, served on the city council, and worked to have Bankhead Highway routed through Douglas County. He also served as mayor four times: 1899, 1900, 1922, and 1930. (Courtesy of the Douglas County Public Library.)

Around the table are, from left to right, Mrs. Wilson, Sara Nell Powell Nicholson, William Hugh "Nick" Nicholson, and Bill Wilson at the Masonic Temple in Atlanta. The Wilsons owned Red Barn Antiques, and the Nicholsons owned The Store in Douglasville. (Courtesy of Carol Musser Nicholson.)

This group of men is celebrating the end of World War II in 1945. From left to right are Roy Lawler, Grover Lee, Paul Umphery, and Roy Marlow. (Courtesy of the City of Douglasville.)

Herman Talmadge came to Douglasville on November 23, 1949, for the Douglas County Progressive Day celebration. He is shown addressing the crowd in the gymnasium of the Douglas County High School. (Courtesy of the City of Douglasville.)

Today, a house sits on this spot, but once, a city swimming pool was located here, south of the current post office on Campbellton Street. (Courtesy of the City of Douglasville.)

This unidentified man poses along Broad Street, between the Douglasville Banking Company and the Crescent Theater, in the 1920s, when gas pumps lined the sidewalk. (Courtesy of the City of Douglasville.)

The McElreath house on Campbellton Street was once situated directly behind today's Precedence, Inc., on the corner of Campbellton and Broad Streets. Serving as a boardinghouse, the home dated back to the 1880s. Census records indicate Robert A. Massey, among others, boarded there through the years. (Courtesy of the City of Douglasville.)

On November 11, 1918, the *Sentinel* wrote, "Douglasville people were aroused from their morning slumber by the ringing of the bells"—bells that signaled the end of World War I, but not before several of Douglasville's finest young men, including Stephen G. Baggett, seen here in his uniform, had marched off to war during the summer of 1917. (Courtesy of Mike Garrett.)

This monument in the Douglasville City Cemetery pays tribute to Cpl. Frank P. Dorris, Douglasville's first casualty of World War I. Dorris was killed in action at Belleau Wood during the Battle of Chateau Thierry in France. Douglasville's American Legion Post No. 145 is named in honor of Dorris. (Author's collection.)

John V. Edge, an attorney and former mayor of Douglasville, built this home in the 1890s. At one time, the home served as a boardinghouse for the shirt and sock factory in town. Herschel Upshaw bought the place in 1902. His brother William D. Upshaw, a presidential candidate in 1932, was a frequent visitor. The Bennett and Sherrod families have also owned the home, respectively. (Courtesy of Frankie Morris.)

N.B. Duncan originally owned this home on Bowden Street. In the late 1880s, he and his brother, J.T., moved their stock into the building at the corner of Pray and Broad Streets, which had previously housed a saloon and, before that, the Skint Chestnut store. N.B. Duncan was very involved in the city government, having served on the city council. (Courtesy of Frankie Morris.)

Douglas County was just three years old when John William "Will" Baggett was born in 1873. Married to Martha Ann "Mattie" Hamby, Baggett served as the Douglas County tax collector during the 1930s. The couple had 11 children: Kate, Guy, Grady, Rufus, Paul, Denman, Pearl, Blanche, Mollie Mae, Faye, and Eunice. (Courtesy of Mike Garrett.)

Built by J.C. McCarley, this home on Campbellton Street was the first in Douglasville to be constructed with brick. Folks were so intrigued they stood in the yard to watch. (Author's collection.)

Going all the way back to Douglasville's earliest days, a Baggett family member has owned a business along Broad or Church Streets, including former sheriff Seawright Baggett and his brother Noah, who operated a hardware store in 1875. This is the interior of the Baggetts' store on Broad Street. Denman Baggett is second from left, and Rufus "Rube" Baggett is fifth from left. (Courtesy of Mike Garrett.)

In 1895, Rena Anderson, a graduate of Douglasville College, married Oscar McNiel in her parents' home, that of Robert and Pellonia Anderson, on Bowden Street. Newspaper accounts advise a rather large crowd attended the ceremony to wish the couple well. (Courtesy of Phyllis Whitfield.)

Seen here with wife Sudie, S.N. Dorsett was very involved in shaping the business and political affairs of Douglasville until he relocated to Louisiana in 1891. Beginning in the 1870s, S.N. held the position of postmaster for Douglasville and was a partner in the dry goods business of Price & McElreath. During the 1880s, he served as clerk of court for Douglas County. (Courtesy of Phyllis Whitfield.)

Pictured here in 1952, Quillian Bonds had a studio on the second floor of the Hutcheson Building, where Gumbeaux's Cajun Café is today on Broad Street. He also took many of the photographs that were published in the *Sentinel* during that time. (Courtesy of the Douglas County Public Library.)

In the early 1950s, a new chapter of the Eastern Star was organized in Douglasville. Gathered for the photograph are, from left to right, (first row) Elma Clements, Lena Houseworth, Lena McKoy, Mrs. Ivor Johnston, Nancy Banks, Essie Lively, Irene Vansant, and Lillie Mae Harrell; (second row) Velma Truett, Queenie Joiner, Lucille Wright, Ruth Siler, Gerila Atkinson, Elizabeth Hunter, Maggie Lou Glover, Dorothy Hamrick, Sarah Greenwood, Dorothy Padgett, Gladys Daniell, Margaret Vansant, Frances Mozley, and Julie Sutton; (third row) Muriel Arnold, Helen Smith, Genelle Moody, Dewitt Glover, James Morris, Murphy Hunter, Quinton Wood, Betty Wood, Dave Padgett, Patsy Smith, Juanita Maupin, William Greenwood, and Betty Abercrombie. (Courtesy of the Douglas County Public Library.)

In 1952, the City of Douglasville participated in the Georgia Power Champion Home Town contest. The aim was to see which city could make the most improvements within one year and win a cash prize. Cleanup campaigns and renovations to many downtown stores were part of Douglasville's strategy. To improve cooperation and neighborliness, a community-wide picnic was held on Monday, July 14, 1952, as seen here at the Veteran's Clubhouse. In addition to a performance by the Douglas County High School band, the event included a square dance, games, skits, and great food. (Courtesy of the Douglas County Pubic Library.)

From the 1940s through the 1960s, Cecil and Agnes Barnett owned the Douglasville Café at the corner of Broad and Campbellton Streets. Their son, O.C., and his wife, Katherine, managed the restaurant, with Katherine and cook Beulah Vance arriving at 5:00 a.m. each morning to serve biscuits to hungry truckers, policemen, and firefighters. (Courtesy of Ed Landers.)

In 1957, the Downtown Merchants Association, led by J. Thad Smith, presented a "turkey fly," in which live turkeys were dropped from the roofs of downtown businesses along Broad Street. Fun and chaos ensued. (Courtesy of Huey and Georgia McIntosh.)

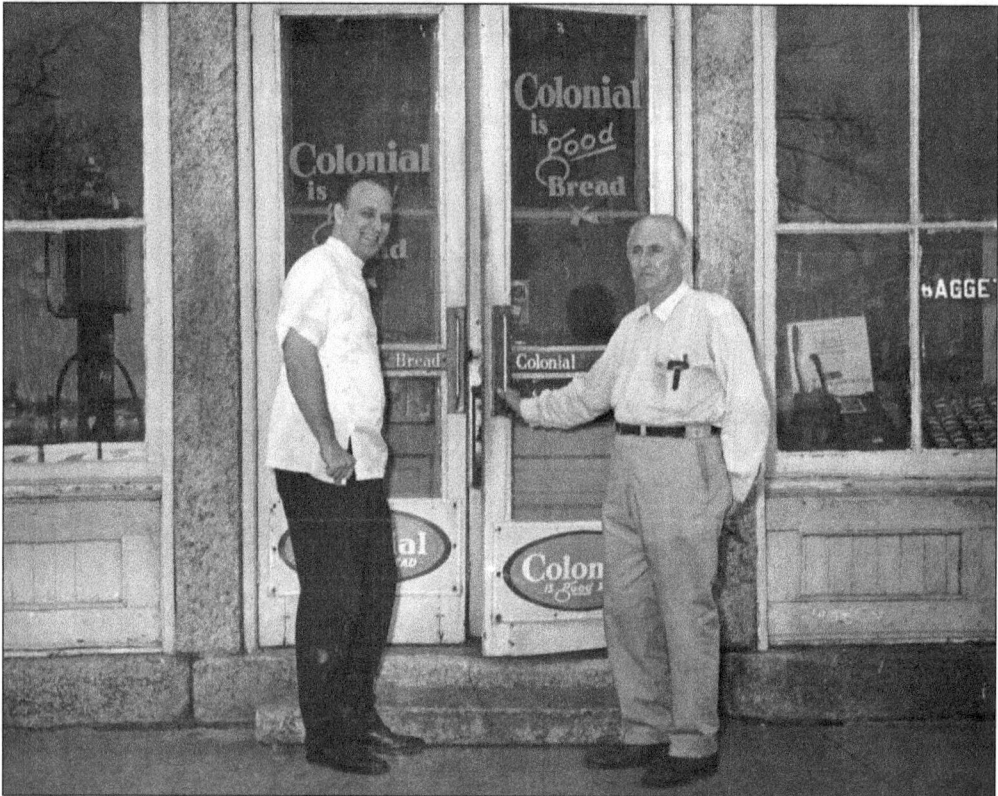

Around 1965, Gwynne Maurer (left), owner of the Church Street Pharmacy, bought the former location of Guy Baggett's store on Broad Street. This photograph was taken the day the keys exchanged hands. Notice the reflection of the old gas pump in the store window at left, one of the last vestiges of vintage Douglasville and the last gas pump along Broad Street to be removed. During the many years that Baggett (right) owned the store, he never missed a day of work. Gwynne Maurer went on to serve as mayor of Douglasville from 1972 to 1975, as chairman of the Douglas County Commission beginning in 1985, and as county representative of the Atlanta Regional Planning Commission. (Courtesy of Douglas County Public Library.)

In 1920, the city of Douglasville celebrated the Fourth of July with a three-day event. According to the *Sentinel*, "There was dancing at the courthouse, there was dinner on the lawn, there was speaking at the grove, and a hot time, sure you're born." J.L. Selman's Drugstore is visible in the background, where the Irish Bred Pub is located today. (Courtesy of the City of Douglasville.)

The Fourth of July celebration also included a baseball game against Acworth in which Douglasville was shut out 6-0, as well as an all-day singing. Dr. T.R. Selman also announced his candidacy for state representative. (Courtesy of the City of Douglasville.)

During the 1940–1941 school year, the FFA sponsored a livestock show and sale in Douglasville, with brood mares and colts, beef and dairy calves, and swine. To kick off the event, the animals and their owners formed a parade in which a total of 79 animals marched through the streets of town. (Courtesy of the Douglas County Library.)

FFA members and Douglas County farmers parade their livestock down Broad Street in downtown Douglasville during the early 1940s. The two-story building with chimneys is now the location of Gumbeaux's Cajun Café. (Courtesy of the Douglas County Public Library.)

From left to right, George Carl Matthews, Dick Butler, and Clay Hindmon are seen along Broad Street, whiling away the afternoon sometime prior to World War I. (Courtesy of the Douglas County Public Library.)

BIBLIOGRAPHY

Albertson, Earl M. *Portraits of History: 1815–1950*. Lithia Springs, GA: Earl M. Albertson, 1998.

Asher & Adams Map of Georgia and Alabama. New York: Asher & Adams, 1872.

Atlanta Journal-Constitution archives.

Cooper, Lisa. *Every Now and Then* [blog]. http://douglascountyhistory.blogspot.com.

Davis, Fannie Mae. *Douglas County, Georgia: From Indian Trail to Interstate 20*. Fernandina, FL: Wolfe Publishing, 1997.

Douglas County Sentinel.

Finley, Anthony. *A New General Atlas, Comprising a Complete Set of Maps, Representing the Grand Divisions of the Globe, Together with the Several Empires, Kingdoms and States in the World*. Philadelphia: Anthony Finley, 1830.

Mitchell, S. Augustus. *Mitchell's New General Atlas, Containing Maps of the Various Countries of the World, Plans of Cities, Etc., Embraced in Seventy-Nine Quarto Maps, Forming a Series of One Hundred and Twelve Maps and Plans, Together with Valuable Statistical Tables*. Philadelphia: S. Augustus Mitchell, 1874.

INDEX

Adair Street, 83, 84
antiques, 89, 92, 93, 112
appliances, 84, 94
attorneys, 75, 77, 93, 98, 100, 108, 109, 116
auto dealers and service stations, 72, 75, 82, 84, 87, 88
Bankhead Highway, 26, 38, 49, 82, 84, 86, 88, 89, 93, 109
banks, 67, 71, 73, 76, 79, 83, 88, 89, 94, 101, 105, 114
beauty shops and barbershops, 28, 66, 73
blacksmith shop, 96,
boardinghouses and hotels, 28, 67, 69, 83, 115, 116
Bowden Street, 15, 17, 35, 37, 66, 71, 95, 109, 117, 119
Broad Street, 13, 18, 19, 36, 46, 58, 65, 66, 68, 70–72, 75–82, 84–88, 91, 93, 95, 99, 101, 103, 111, 114, 115, 117, 118, 121–125
bus station and taxi services, 83, 84
Campbellton Street, 36, 50, 55, 58, 65, 79, 84, 88, 97, 98, 100, 102, 114, 115, 118, 121
cemetery, 106, 116
Chicago Avenue, 50, 107, 111
Church Street, 18, 25, 35, 37, 38, 40, 41, 45–48, 51, 73, 74, 83, 90, 91, 95, 96, 105, 118, 122
churches, 46–49, 52, 53, 56, 101, 102
Colquitt Street, 108
cotton gin, mill, and warehouse, 25–35, 49, 80, 105, 106, 108
Douglas County Courthouse, 11–19, 31, 48, 56, 95, 107, 108, 119
Douglas County government, 10–12, 14–19, 43, 45, 73, 94, 103, 117
Douglas County Sentinel, 71, 87, 120
Douglas County sheriff, 40, 41, 94, 112, 118
Douglasville City Council, 36, 38, 39, 70, 87, 104, 112, 117
Douglasville City Hall, 36–38, 42, 67, 81, 90
Douglasville police, 37, 38, 42, 87

drugstores, 37, 66, 68, 93, 122, 123
dry goods and mercantile stores, 65, 66, 70, 72, 75, 78, 104, 119
dry cleaners, 91, 92
factories and refining companies, 74, 85, 93
fire, 17, 21, 34, 67
Fourth of July, 79, 98, 123
Forrest Avenue, 58
funeral home, 96
Future Farmers of America, 55, 58, 63, 64, 86, 124
grocery stores, 28, 76, 77, 79, 88, 89, 99, 112, 122
Highway 92/Fairburn Road, 31, 33, 41, 43, 74, 85, 88
hospital and physicians, 31, 43–46, 74, 105
Huey Road, 106
Malone Street, 69
Masons, 74, 101
mayor, 35–39, 42, 70, 76, 87, 98–100, 108, 112, 116, 122
McCarley Street, 84
movie theater, 67, 76, 81, 90, 114
mule barn, 94, 95
O'Neal Plaza, 67, 81, 90
post office, 23, 50, 66, 74, 77, 106, 107, 119
Prestley Mill Road, 46, 47
Price Avenue, 46, 73, 74, 81, 83, 90, 93, 104
Pray Street, 11, 38, 49, 56, 72, 85, 117
railroad, 20–24
restaurants, 68, 76–78, 82, 85, 86, 93, 107, 120, 121, 123, 124
Rose Avenue, 46, 95, 106
saloon, 72, 117
schools, 31, 43, 50–64, 100, 103, 104, 113, 121
Skint Chestnut, 9, 11, 12, 20, 72, 117
Spring Street, 45, 50
Strickland Street, 28, 50, 69, 84, 86, 105, 108
Weekly Star, 66, 102

Visit us at
arcadiapublishing.com

www.ingramcontent.com/pod-product-compliance
Lightning Source LLC
Chambersburg PA
CBHW080621110426
42813CB00006B/1569